Integrating QS-9000 with Your Automotive Quality System

Also available from ASQC Quality Press

Preparing Your Company for QS-9000: A Guide for the Automotive Industry, Second Edition
Richard Clements, Stanley M. Sidor, and Rand E. Winters Jr.

IASG Sanctioned QS-9000 Interpretations
International Automotive Sector Group

After the Quality Audit: Closing the Loop on the Audit Process
J. P. Russell and Terry Regel

Managing Records for ISO 9000 Compliance
Eugenia K. Brumm

The ISO 9000 Auditor's Companion and *The Audit Kit*
Kent A. Keeney

Statistical Process Control for Long and Short Runs, Second Edition
Gary K. Griffith

Failure Mode and Effect Analysis: FMEA from Theory to Execution
D. H. Stamatis

To request a complimentary catalog of publications,
call 800-248-1946.

Integrating QS-9000 with Your Automotive Quality System

Second Edition

D. H. Stamatis

ASQC Quality Press
Milwaukee, Wisconsin

Integrating QS-9000 with Your Automotive Quality System
D. H. Stamatis

Library of Congress Cataloging-in-Publication Data

Stamatis, D. H., 1947–
    Integrating QS-9000 with your automotive quality system / D. H.
Stamatis—2nd ed.
        p.   cm.
    Includes bibliographical references and index.
    ISBN 0-87389-408-1 (alk. paper)
        1. Automobile industry and trade—United States—Quality control—
Standards.   2. QS-9000 (Standard).   I. Title.
TL278.S72   1996
629.23'068—dc20   96-18493
                                                              CIP

10 9 8 7 6 5 4 3 2 1

ISBN 0-87389-408-1

Acquisitions Editor: Roger Holloway
Project Editor: Jeanne W. Bohn

ASQC Mission: To facilitate continuous improvement and increase customer satisfaction by identifying, communicating, and promoting the use of quality principles, concepts, and technologies; and thereby be recognized throughout the world as the leading authority on, and champion for, quality.

Attention: Schools and Corporations
ASQC Quality Press books, audiotapes, videotapes, and software are available at quantity discounts with bulk purchases for business, educational, or instructional use. For information, please contact ASQC Quality Press at 800-248-1946, or write to ASQC Quality Press, P.O. Box 3005, Milwaukee, WI 53201-3005.

For a free copy of the ASQC Quality Press Publications Catalog, including ASQC membership information, call 800-248-1946.

Printed in the United States of America

 Printed on acid-free paper

Quality Press
611 East Wisconsin Avenue
Milwaukee, Wisconsin 53202

In memory of my grandparents
Diomidi, Sotiria,
Aristidi, and Paraskeve

Contents

Figures and Tables

Figures

Tables

Preface

With the proliferation of the ISO 9000 family of standards throughout the world, including the United States, the automotive industry on its own has developed a quality system that is based on the ISO 9001 structure. This system is capable of satisfying the international standards and the individual company's product requirements, and at the same time can provide a harmonization of all the standards and the collective requirements of their supplier base. The system is found in *Quality System Requirements: QS-9000*.

In its entirety, QS-9000 was developed to standardize the fundamental supplier quality systems manuals and assessment tools. The system became effective on September 1, 1994, and its spirit is continuous improvement. It was revised in February 1995.

It is hoped that this quality system will be accepted worldwide, will enhance quality in general, and will eliminate redundant requirements, consequently reducing costs. In the process, prevention will be emphasized throughout the organization (both internal and external) with the ultimate result being that variation and waste in the supply chain will be minimized, if not completely eliminated.

QS-9000 specifically replaces Chrysler's *Supplier Quality Assurance Manual,* General Motors' North America Operation's *Targets for Excellence,* and Ford's *Q-101 Quality System Standard* with input from some of the truck manufacturers. The base of the standard is ISO 9001:1994 Section 4. However, additional requirements are included and the words *may, should,* and *shall* continue to have the same semantic definition as in ISO 9001 proper. QS-9000 applies to all internal and external suppliers of production, service parts, and materials. In addition, it applies to design-responsible suppliers.

The QS-9000 quality system, as a replacement of the individualized systems, now becomes the major driver of the supplier's quality system, which must conform to the prescribed requirements. As a consequence, conformance to the system will be handled through a third-party registration. The scope of this registration must include all products and services being applied to one or more of the companies subscribing to QS-9000.

This book is about the QS-9000 quality system. It will address the evolution and rationale of the ISO standards (in a cursory manner), its structure, the interpretation of each of the elements, and its relationship to the automotive world. It will discuss a detailed approach for the implementation of the QS-9000 system, using the project management approach, and will identify the documentation structure of the QS-9000 system.

The book is written with two basic objectives in mind. The first is to provide a reference for the QS-9000 material. As a result, the target audience is viewed as anyone who is interested in and/or involved with quality issues in the automotive industry. The second objective is to provide the specific application method(s) and tool(s) of the implementation process of the ISO. This will result in attaining the certification as well as keeping it. The target audience here is viewed as the individual(s) in any organization who is responsible for the implementation process.

The QS-9000 requirement was less than a year old when a new revision was introduced. To be sure, the revision was not a major one, but it enhances the understanding of the entire document. Specifically, the revisions take into account 50 changes. They include

- Three changes in updating
- Four changes in corrections
- Eleven changes in additions
- Fourteen changes in clarifications
- Three changes in deletions
- One change in modification
- Thirteen changes in revisions

The focus of the 1995 revision was to clarify the original document, and the changes were effective immediately. However, those suppliers that have already started their process toward certification based on the August 1994 edition had until January 1996 to update their quality system to meet the current requirements.

The second edition of this book reflects the updated changes and a need to keep current with the expectations of the automotive companies in reference to meeting their quality requirements. For the most part the original text remains intact; however, major changes have been incorporated in updating the review of the QS-9000 introductory material, Figure 1.4, Tables 1.1 and 3.1, and Chapter 4. I also have expanded the QS-9000 implementation process in Chapter 5 as well as the cost of implementation. In addition I have added two new appendixes to reflect the need for a cursory understanding of the most demanding references on the QS-9000 document. The new Appendix C addresses the components and sequence of the production part approval process (PPAP), and Appendix D addresses the issues and concerns of advanced product quality planning (APQP).

How to Use This Book

This book is designed to give readers a complete overview of QS-9000. Toward that end I have provided a cursory background of the historical perspective of automotive quality as well as a complete overview of ISO 9000, the registration process, third-party assessment, and a training curriculum that an organization may use to bring its company under the guidelines of both the ISO 9000 and QS-9000 requirements. This book will help readers get a better understanding of what is required to get the certification.

Acknowledgments

Many people have contributed to the production of this book, either directly or indirectly.

I want to thank, as always, my chief editor, my motivator, and the one who helped make this book possible through so many ways. This person is my wife, Carla.

I want to thank my children, Christine, Cary, Stephen, and Timothy, for the patience they showed during my long writing days, without complaining, even though I have a sense that they were disappointed when I missed most of their soccer games and high school band competitions during the late summer and early fall of 1994 when I was writing the first edition.

I want to thank the Automotive Task Force of Chrysler Corporation, Ford Motor Company, and General Motors Corporation, as well as the AIAG, for granting me permission to use the documentation progression in Figure 4.1.

I want to thank ASQC for granting me permission to quote from the ANSI/ISO/ASQC A8402-1994 vocabulary standard.

I want to thank Ms. E. Rice and Mr. R. Munro for their thoughtful suggestions and encouragement throughout the project.

I want to specially thank Mr. G. A. Schembri for his valuable contribution to the automotive section of Chapter 4.

I want to thank Mr. H. Jamal and Ms. D. Fletcher for their continuous support, encouragement, reviewing earlier drafts, suggestions, and help with the typing and the computer graphics. Without them, this project would not have progressed. Their help was greatly appreciated.

Special thanks also belong to the reviewers of ASQC Quality Press, as well as the editors, for their thoughtful suggestions and recommendations to make this a better book.

Finally, I want to thank all the participants of my public seminars for offering suggestions and specific recommendations; I have tried to incorporate as many as I could. Without their comments and their input this book would not have been possible.

CHAPTER 1

A General Introduction to Quality Standards

This chapter's focus is to address the issue of quality standards and to demonstrate that the concept is not new by summarizing some of the historical facts of quality. While standards and certification procedures have been around for a long time, the difference between the past and present is that the current certification process is more sophisticated and can be replicated on a more consistent basis. In addition, I will provide an overview of the ISO standards and discuss the need for such standards not only in Europe, but also in the United States and the world markets. Finally, the QS-9000 quality requirements for the automotive industry will be introduced.

Overview of the History of Quality Standards

As defined by ANSI/ISO/ASQC A8402-1994, *quality* is the "totality of characteristics of an entity that bear on its ability to satisfy stated and implied needs." However, whose needs does the service or product address? Who are its customers? How do we define these needs? The questions are not easy to answer. In fact, six notes follow the definition of quality, including, "in a contractual environment . . . needs are specified, whereas in other environments,

1

implied needs should be identified and defined" and that "needs can change with time."

Within this definition, we can identify ideas of fitness for purpose, value for money, reliability, customer satisfaction, environmental impact, versatility, compatibility with other products, maintainability, conformance to requirements, or other desired characteristics. These concepts of quality are not new, nor are they restricted to any age or culture. For some examples of historical perspective on standards and certification see Stamatis 1995, Johnson and Green 1993, Allcock and Unsworth 1991, Goetz 1973, Meek 1973, Corns 1968, Guerdan 1956, and Durant 1954.

As old as the concepts of quality are, it was during the First World War that quality took to the air and caused the Royal Aircraft Establishment to try to improve the reliability of British engines in a systematic methodology. The concern of the British at the time was that when an enemy engine failed, the prevailing wind usually allowed the pilot to return behind his own lines to fight another day; whereas the Allied pilot forced into the same action finished the war as a prisoner.

After the armistice, there was a significant change in the scale and diversity of industry in general. Companies evolved from small, self-contained units into integrated operations where individuals no longer had total control over the end product. Individuals were now responsible for a specific part, which would then be passed from operator to operator or firm to firm, gathering other components on the way to completion.

Another change was the introduction of inspectors who, independent of the manufacturing operations, would assess the work and return any part that was defective for rectification. The introduction of rework and reinspection was here to stay. For many years this iterative process of make, inspect, then accept or rework has been the basis of the manufacturing industry. It is only recently that the more efficient and cost-effective concept of getting it right the first time every time has started to replace it. The further expansion in industrial and technological change, which was started during the Second World War, saw an increase in complexity in the manufacturing process and of its products.

The first attempt to standardize quality was in the United States, where expansion and its effects were greatest and the most significant. This standardization gave rise to MIL-Q-9858 (Military Specification 1956), which is a quality system specification, and MIL-I-45208, which specifies inspection system requirements. Both standards are still current and are utilized in U.S. defense contracts and elsewhere (Duncan 1986).

These two standards formed the basis for a series of standards designed for use within the North Atlantic Treaty Organization (NATO). These were called the Allied Quality Assurance Publications (AQAPs) 1, 4, and 9. Of these, AQAP-1 was a quality system specification and AQAP-4 and AQAP-9 were inspection system specifications. The former covered manufacturing, inspection, and testing, and the latter covered final inspection only (Levy 1993). Despite its membership in NATO, the United Kingdom did not accept the AQAPs. Instead, it introduced a series of three similar specifications, which were called defense standards, or Def. Stans.

The most significant difference between the defense standards and the AQAPs was the introduction of some requirements for design to the quality system specification Def. Stan. 05-21, which otherwise compared with AQAP-1. The other two defense standards were 05-24 and 05-29, which were inspection system standards and covered the same subject matter as AQAP-4 and AQAP-9, respectively (Breitenberg 1993).

Companies engaged in defense contracts and companies that served as subcontractors to defense contractors were assessed by the Ministry of Defense. Companies that complied with the requirements of the appropriate defense standards were registered. In theory, only registered firms could be used on defense contracts.

This is an example of second-party assessment, because only two parties, the company and the ministry, are involved and approval only indicates fitness to meet Ministry of Defense requirements. At a later date the AQAPs were aligned with the defense standards and, progressively, Ministry of Defense assessments have been aligned to the AQAP standards, making the defense standards obsolete.

The AQAPs are very militaristic in their content and wording and make considerable use of that often misunderstood word *materiel,* on which many quality managers' reputations for literacy have floundered. In fact, it is a perfectly proper word that was introduced in France during the Napoleonic Wars to indicate everything necessary to fight a battle or wage a war except the men and horses. By extension, it now refers to everything needed to run a business except the personnel.

Within industry at large there was also a need for quality standards to work. Early attempts to meet this need in the United Kingdom resulted in standards such as BS 4891 and BS 5179. These were in the nature of codes of practice and had no application in contractual situations. The solution that came forth in 1979 was the first edition of BS 5750 (a new version became effective in 1987). This standard was firmly based on AQAPs 1, 4, and 9, and was in three parts. These parts mirrored the AQAPs closely, even to the extent of Part 1 being a quality system specification and Parts 2 and 3 being inspection system specifications. Like the AQAPs, these standards were very subjective and contained a large number of explanatory, nonmandatory notes. Also, as in the AQAPs, Parts 1, 2, and 3 were supported by commentaries, called Parts 4, 5, and 6, which contained interpretive material.

This first version of BS 5750 was not only used in a contractual sense between buyer and seller, but as a third-party registration scheme whereby an independent organization could register companies complying with the requirements of the appropriate part of the standard on behalf of all customers, actual and potential.

The situation that has been described for the United Kingdom existed to a greater or lesser extent throughout the world. As a result, a committee of the International Organization for Standardization or ISO, under the leadership of Canada, worked to produce an international quality standard. The ISO committee considered many national inputs and, in 1987, produced a series of standards that were largely based on BS 5750 and its notes and commentaries. This series is called the ISO 9000 series, which embraces ISO 9001, ISO 9002, ISO 9003, and ISO 9004. The following documents are in the ISO 9000 series.

ISO 9000-1, *Quality management and quality assurance standards—Part 1: Guidelines for selection and use*

ISO 9000-2, *Quality management and quality assurance standards—Part 2: Generic guidelines for the application of ISO 9001, ISO 9002 and ISO 9003*

ISO 9000-3, *Quality management and quality assurance standards—Part 3: Guidelines for the application of ISO 9001 to the development, supply and maintenance of software*

ISO 9001, *Quality systems—Model for quality assurance in design, development, production, installation and servicing*

ISO 9002, *Quality systems—Model for quality assurance in production, installation and servicing*

ISO 9003, *Quality systems—Model for quality assurance in final inspection and test*

ISO 9004-1, *Quality management and quality system elements—Part 1: Guidelines*

ISO 9004-2, *Quality management and quality system elements—Part 2: Guidelines for services*

ISO 10011-1, *Guidelines for auditing quality systems—Part 1: Auditing*

ISO 10011-2, *Guidelines for auditing quality systems—Part 2: Qualification criteria for quality systems auditors*

ISO 10011-3, *Guidelines for auditing quality systems—Part 3: Management of audit programmes*

ISO 10012-1, *Quality assurance requirements for measuring equipment—Part 1: Metrological confirmation system for measuring equipment*

ISO 10013, *Guidelines for developing quality manuals*

ISO 8402, *Quality management and quality assurance— Vocabulary*

Not all these standards are contractual standards. In fact, most of them are considered to be guidelines and aids for the quality system. The certifiable standards are ISO 9001, ISO 9002, and ISO 9003. These are the standards with which most people associate when discussing ISO 9000. There are several outstanding features about the ISO 9000 series certifiable standards.

- It is obvious that they have been produced by people who are acquainted with the problems and failures that occur in industry. The clauses address these points in a manner that is largely objective.

- There are 21 notes in the standard. These are nonmandatory. Their intent is to help the reader understand or clarify the particular clause of the standard. There are no supplementary commentaries.

- Although there are three standards, each is a specification for a quality system. This is in contrast to the three parts of BS 5750, which are progressive and additive.

    No longer is there a quantum leap from Parts 2 and 3 to Part 1. If the requirements for the production process are added to those of Part 3 and some very minor changes are made to the wording, Part 2 results. If the requirements for design/development and servicing are added to these with similar changes to words, the standard is converted to Part 1.

- There is little dictation in the standards. Only rarely do they prescribe a condition. Often, the standards require the company to establish its own procedures.

- While the standards originally pertained to the metal cutting industry, they now can be applied, with minimal interpretation, to any industry. Some diverse examples include food, automotive, electronics, medical device, and service industries.

- Although ISO 9004-1 addresses quality-related cost considerations and product safety and liability, there is no reference to these topics in any of the current operating standards. However, plans for their inclusion in future editions are well underway. Examples are in the area of safety, reliability, product liability, cost of quality, and others.

Although there has been widespread acceptance of ISO 9000 throughout the world, the third-party application of it varies widely. The United Kingdom, in 1993, had the most extensive third-party registration system in the world—more British companies were registered by third parties than in any other country. The United Kingdom's share at the time was nearly 67 percent of the worldwide total. At the same time, Japan had no national third-party registration and the United States with Canada had only 4.3 percent of the worldwide total. As of December 1, 1994, according to CEEM Information Services, the United States had increased its number of registered companies to 4942 (7 percent of the 70,517 worldwide), and Canada's number reached 1020 (1.4 percent) (CEEM 1995; Morrow 1995). As of this writing the United Kingdom still holds the lead in registered companies with 52 percent of all registrations (Morrow 1995).

Many other countries have approved, instituted, or set up third-party registration systems with national recognition. Some countries, such as Pakistan, Zambia, Brunei, Malta, Costa Rica, Iceland, and Bahrain, have either a single registration or fewer than five issued certificates. Other countries, such as Belgium, Denmark, Italy, India, Hong Kong, Singapore, Brazil, South Africa, and the Netherlands, have shown significant growth in registration activity.

It should be noted that one country, for example the United Kingdom, may register companies from other countries because those companies want to trade in the United Kingdom and find that registration by a British organization is advantageous. Mutual recognition of one country's registration system by another is being extensively and increasingly negotiated, but progress is slow and, in many cases, complicated. As of this writing the Registrar Accreditation Board (RAB) does not have a full reciprocity with many countries. However, RAB is working diligently toward this end and it is expected that reciprocity will in fact be secured before long. The significance of reciprocity is that by recognizing each other's certification, the registrars will create a more standardized quality system for all concerned.

In 1991, there were 15 independent bodies in the United Kingdom assessing companies worldwide on their ability to meet the requirements of ISO 9001, 9002, or 9003, and registering those who did. A common standard of assessment is ensured by a body set up under the auspices of the government's Department of Trade and Industry called the United Kingdom Accreditation System (UKAS), formerly the National Accreditation Council for Certification Bodies (NACCB). More bodies are awaiting accreditation as certifying organizations.

The five largest, which have the scope to undertake assessments of companies in a wide range of industries in the world markets, including the United States, are the following:

- British Standards Institution (BSI) Quality Assurance. This is a commercial company that receives no public funding. It is associated only with the partially publicly funded standards (making and selling) organization at the highest administrative level.

- Bureau Veritas Quality International.

- Lloyds Register Quality Assurance.

- Det Norske Veritas Quality Assurance Ltd.

  (These four accredited certifying bodies each have their origin in a well-established, internationally operating, third-party inspection organization.)

- Yarsley Quality Assured Firms Limited. This is an assessment organization that derives from the Institute of Physics via the Fulmer and Yarsley laboratories.

In the United States the list of registrars is increasing. Some are

- AT&T

- Entela Quality System Registration Division

- Quality Systems Registrar

- Underwriter Laboratory

- Perry Johnson

- Automotive QSR (specializing in automotive)

For a complete and up-to-date list of all the registrars the reader is encouraged to contact RAB (U.S. phone number 800-248-1946).

In addition to the general registrars, specific registrars exist to assess companies in specific areas of activity such as steel reinforcing, electrical wiring, construction and ceramics, and automotive. Specialization seems to be the way of the future, with each major industry adapting some of the specific applications of the standards to its own needs. These organizations are in commercial competition with one another, and, although the UKAS ensures that common standards are applied, the details of the method and fees vary from one to another.

Not only have the standards in the ISO 9000–9004 series been accepted in the national systems of many countries throughout the world, they have been adopted as Euronormes by the European Union and numbered EN 29000–29004. Consequently, one standard was designated as a British (BS 5750, Part 1:1987), European (EN 29001: 1987), and international (ISO 9001:1987) standard. [In the British system ISO 9000-1 and ISO 9004-1 (EN 29000 and 29004) have been combined into a single standard, BS 5750: Part 0, Sections 0.1 and 0.2, respectively.]

In the United States, the ISO 9000 quality system has been named the Q9000 quality system. The only difference between the ISO 9000 and Q9000 is that the Q9000 standards are written in American English. The contents, requirements, and philosophy are exactly the same for both systems. The introduction of the automotive requirements named QS-9000 is strictly an American innovation and, as of this writing, applies only to the United States. However, all the U.S. companies plan to use QS-9000 both internally (in their own plants) and externally (with their suppliers in the United States, Europe, Asia, and everywhere else they do business). What characterizes QS-9000 as a quality system is that the basic flavor of the ISO 9001 is kept as originally intended; however, additional requirements have been added to satisfy the specifics of the automotive industry.

In 1990, BSI introduced BS 5750: Part 4: 1990 entitled *Guide to the Use of BS 5750: Part 1, Part 2 and Part 3.* This standard is exclusive to the United Kingdom and it is essential that it not be confused with ISO 9004. It has no relationship to any ISO standard.

It has already been said that BS 5750: 1979 was very subjective and that considerable guidance was needed for its use. In addition to the textual notes and the commentaries, further guidance was given by BSI's quality assessment schedules, Bureau Veritas Quality International's quality standard supplements, and Lloyds' quality system supplements. Each was oriented toward a particular industry and contained additional requirements relevant to that industry or gave information on how the standard was to be understood in that industry. Since production of the 1987 standard, a number of bodies representing sectors of industry have produced guidelines on the use of the standard within that industry. Examples are

- *BS 5750: Guidelines for Use by the Chemical Industry,* published by the Chemical Industries Association Ltd.

- *Guidelines for the Use of BS 5750: Part 2: 1987 in the Manufacture of Food and Drink,* published by the Leatherhead Food Research Association

- *Quality Assurance, Cleansing Services, Grounds Maintenance and Leisure Facilities,* a guidance document on the use of BS 5750: 1987, published by the local government sector quality committee of the British Quality Association

- *Quality systems—Guide to quality management services,* produced in July 1988 as a draft guide, reference ISO/TC176/SC2/WG6 by the International Organization for Standardization

The guidelines do not change the requirements of the standard but they indicate to the user the points relevant or peculiar to the industry that must be considered under each clause of the standard.

The policy of the British Ministry of Defense (MOD) toward third-party assessments to ISO 9001 and ISO 9002 has been defined in *Special Bulletin* (1/90) issued by the director general of defense quality assurance in July 1990. This says that the MOD will continue to require compliance with the appropriate AQAP, but it is now prepared to accept certification to the relevant ISO standard as being adequate for that purpose.

From September 1, 1991, suppliers of products or services for which there is a quality control/inspection requirement shall be certified by an accredited body as a prerequisite to entry on the defense contractors list. This certification must be maintained for a company to remain on the list.

The MOD reserved the right to carry out assessments after that date and to specify the conditions under which it would do so. These assessments are undertaken according to ISO specifications, not the AQAPs, except in the case of companies in which software supply is a major consideration. AQAP-1 and its software-specific counterpart, AQAP-13, will be the basis of assessment in that case.

Introduction to the ISO 9000 Series Standards

The ISO 9000 series standards were developed by the International Organization for Standardization, a Geneva, Switzerland, organization founded in 1946 to promote the development of international standards and related activities, including conformity assessment (testing, inspection, laboratory accreditation, certification, quality system assessment, and other activities intended to ensure the conformity of products to a set of standards and/or technical specifications), to facilitate the exchange of goods and services worldwide. The organization chose *iso* as the prefix for its numerical standards because it comes from the Greek root *iso,* which means *equal.* It is not an acronym for the International Organization for Standardization, though the organization does use ISO as the shortened version of its name.

ISO is composed of nearly 200 technical committees and its members are from over 90 countries, with the U.S. member being the American National Standards Institute (ANSI). The jurisdiction of the standards extends to all areas except those related to electrical and electronics engineering, which are covered by the International Electrotechnical Commission (IEC). The results of ISO's technical work are published as international standards or guides. Technical Committee 176 (ISO/TC 176) on Quality Management and Quality Assurance began working in 1979 on the ISO 9000 series standards, which were first approved in 1987.

Detailed descriptions of the development of the standards has been given elsewhere in the literature (Peach 1992; Lamprecht 1992; Cottman 1993; MacLean 1993; Bureau of Business Practice 1992; Voehl, Jackson, and Ashton 1994) and, as such, in this section a limited overview will be given in a pictorial format through Figure 1.1, Figure 1.2, and Figure 1.3. Figure 1.1 shows the evolution of the ISO 9000 series standards, Figure 1.2 shows the development of the standards, and Figure 1.3 shows the ISO 9000 certification hierarchy.

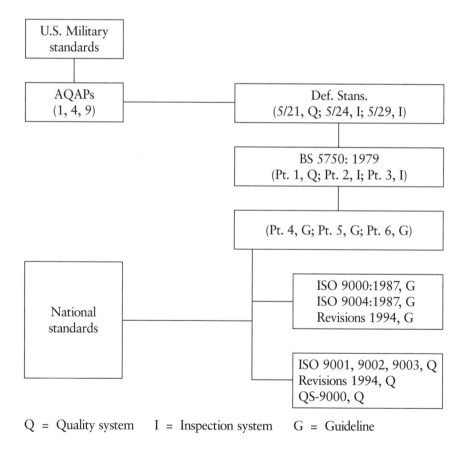

Q = Quality system   I = Inspection system   G = Guideline

Figure 1.1. Evolution of the ISO 9000 series standards.

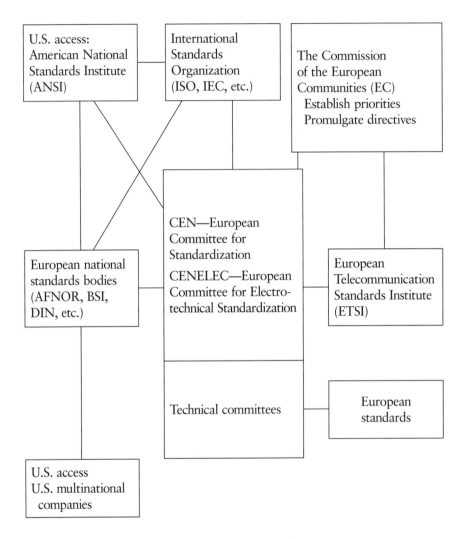

Figure 1.2. Development of European standards.

As we have seen, the ISO 9000 series is a result of an evolutionary process and is primarily composed of five documents (ISO 9000-1, 9001, 9002, 9003, and 9004-1). The series describes three quality standards, defines quality concepts, and gives guidelines for

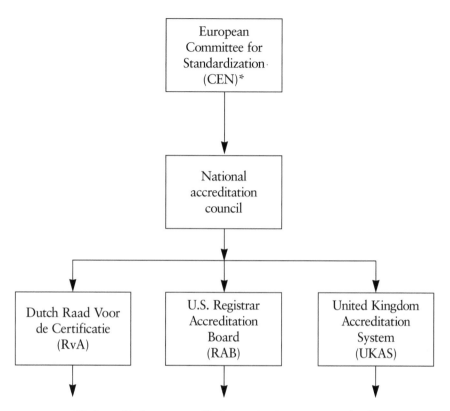

Various third-party certified organizations are accredited
by one or all of these three organizations.

*CEN members are national standardization organizations.

Figure 1.3. The ISO 9000 certification hierarchy.

using international standards on quality systems. Contrary to what
many believe, ISO 9000 does not apply to specific products and
does not guarantee that a manufacturer produces a *quality* product
(Stamatis 1992). The standards are generic and enable a company
to ensure (by means of internal and external third-party audits) that
it has a quality system in place that meets one of the three published
standards for a quality system.

An issue usually discussed in relation to ISO is the question, "Why the ISO standard?" The answer is a multiple one. However, fundamentally it has to do with the creation of the single western European market. Twelve separate markets, after long international negotiations, became one. Most barriers to free movement of goods (free trade) are being removed. This fact alone presents an unprecedented level of opportunities, but considerable changes for the organizations that want to participate. To effectively trade with each other and be assured that goods and services meet a consistent set of standards, agreed-upon quality standards had to be developed or accepted within the community. The impetus for international standards was created by this movement toward a free market.

The European market is made up of 18 countries—12 from the European Union (EU), representing 320 million consumers, and six from the European Free Trade Association (EFTA) representing 30 million consumers. Table 1.1 identifies the member countries. By contrast, the United States and Japan represent 250 million and 120 million consumers, respectively (Hagigh 1992). The EU countries have developed bridging agreements and have agreed to 76 technical directives to enable the formation of this free trade market. The European Committee for Standardization (CEN) was mandated to develop harmonized versions of the ISO 9000 series standards, which are designated EN 29000. All 16 member nations of CEN must adopt EN 29000 as national standards.

The standardization has had a profound effect in the United States since the European Union (previously known as the European Community) was formed and became one of the United States' premier customers (Linville 1992). In 1993 the United States exported $464 billion in goods and services, and as of November 1994 the United States exported $465 billion in goods and services. As such, the United States has a tremendous interest in the world market (Trade Adjustment Assistance Centers 1995).

Table 1.1. The European market.

European Union (EU)	European Free Trade Association (EFTA)	Consumers (millions)
Austria	Finland	350
Denmark	Iceland	
Germany	Norway	
Greece	Sweden	
Ireland	Switzerland	
Italy		
Luxembourg		
Netherlands		
Portugal		
Spain		
United Kingdom		

To date, 91 countries that have signed an agreement to abide by these standards.

In the United States the movement for standardization has gained ground in several industries such as steel, chemical, automotive, electronics, software, and the federal government. The goal of this fast-paced movement is to allow individual organizations and governmental agencies the opportunity to

- Define the quality system that is appropriate and applicable to a given organization

- Demonstrate to the customers the commitment and management system to maintain quality

- Compete in the international markets

- Follow standard safety and product liability regulations and/or procedures

- Reduce cost and provide a practical results-oriented target(s)

- Maintain quality improvement gains

- Minimize supplier surveillance through second-party audits

- Provide a platform from which to launch a continuous improvement program such as total quality management (TQM), the Malcolm Baldrige National Quality Award, and so on

- Involve all employees by stimulating understanding of quality systems

Advantages of Following ISO Standards

- Following a standard can lead to greater profit. Poor quality costs British industry some 10 billion pounds each year. Typically, the cost of not finding out what the customer needs and then meeting those requirements faultlessly, every time, is costing companies 15 percent to 50 percent of sales. The average profit made by a British company is 4 percent of sales, and any reduction in quality costs goes straight to profits. Companies operating good quality management systems can reduce quality costs below 5 percent of sales (Allcock and Unsworth 1991).

  In the United States these costs have been estimated to be anywhere from 10 percent to 50 percent of gross sales. Improvements have been made in cost of quality in various industries and published results have shown that some individual companies operate as low as 3 percent of their gross sales (Crosby 1985).

- Staff members can be more motivated for a number of reasons.

  —Employees are not being continually harassed to perform rework and still meet the deadline. Nor are they on the receiving end of the customer's wrath.

  —The standard requires procedures to be established. By getting the workforce involved, members are committed to these standards.

—Through its independent audit and management review clauses, the standard opens beneficial horizontal and vertical lines of communication.

—The standard requires corrective actions to be identified, taken, and verified as effective. Because the ongoing surveillance activity ensures that these requirements are complied with, frustration is eliminated.

—Increased profitability is conducive to job security.

• When approved and registered, the details of the company appear in the Department of Trade and Industry's register of approved firms and are also circulated by the certifying body (for example, BSI publishes this information in its monthly newsletter and in its annual buyer's guide). All these publications have a wide and general circulation and can bring additional business to registered firms by bringing their abilities to the attention of potential customers.

• Registered companies are permitted to use a logo announcing their registration in a wide range of circumstances, including in their advertising (though the logo may not be used in any manner to deceive or imply that a *product* is approved). This can also attract new business.

It must be noted that registration to an ISO standard applies only to the *quality system* that the company operates. The third party ensures that a *product* conforms to its appropriate standard or manufacturing or performance regulations and then allows use of its mark (such as the BSI kite mark or safety mark, the Health and Safety Executive's BASEEFA mark, British Telecom's green disc, and various other marks issued by a variety of organizations). The operation of a quality system registered to ISO 9000 is a prerequisite of some product marks; for example, BSI's kite mark.

- Although not yet proven by case law, there is a strong consensus of legal opinion that a disciplined quality management system, according to the relevant ISO 9000 standard and the maintenance of records that the standard requires, will provide the best possible plea of mitigation in any product liability case. Many insurance companies providing product liability indemnity policies offer reduced premiums to registered organizations (Kokla and Scott 1992).

- Registration to ISO 9000 is a necessary prerequisite to supply to a growing number of government, national, and private organizations.

- The ISO equivalence of the standard gives international recognition of ability.

Disadvantages of Following ISO Standards

- The implementation of a formal quality system is very demanding of resources. Although it is improbable that any company that has traded successfully in a competitive market for any length of time is without a system, the formalization and documentation of the system is time-consuming and may involve considerable clerical expense. Assessment and registration are costly.

- Unless carefully planned, the system can become costly and burdensome.

- By exposing people's actions and cherished practices as not conducive to quality, the process can become traumatic.

- The need to change attitudes and get employees to accept new working practices may strain management's capability beyond its ability to manage.

- Although registration of a company to ISO 9000 is often expected to eliminate second-party assessment, this does not occur in practice. It is possible that more purchasers will accept the standard as the sole qualification for a supplier as it becomes better known and more widespread. However, it is more likely that it will be used as a guide to indicate those companies that are worth looking at more closely.

Introduction to the QS-9000 Quality System

Automotive quality has always been important in the United States. The degree of that quality commitment, however, may indeed be argued. In the early 1980s, the quality revolution came to the automotive world and the race to be the best began with a relentless introduction of programs and methodologies to improve products, customer satisfaction, and supplier relations. This revolution created a monster of standards, policies, and procedures to individualized that, for all intents and purposes, the focus became the paperwork rather than the quality of the product. The individualized standards and policies were beginning to choke the supplier base.

Something had to be done. Chrysler Corporation, Ford Motor Company, and General Motors Corporation (GM), known as the "Big Three," started to talk about harmonizing the requirements. The talks resulted in the formation of the Chrysler, Ford, and General Motors Supplier Quality Requirements Task Force— known simply as the Task Force, which is the body responsible for developing the guidelines, requirements, and the harmonization of the supplier quality processes. In 1995, the Task Force started developing officially sanctioned QS-9000 interpretations. The Task Force is the developing body, but the Automotive Industry Action Group (AIAG) was given the responsibility to distribute and act as the clearinghouse of all the documents that the Task Force develops and coordinate all the approved QS-9000 training for North America. It must be clearly understood that the role and function of the Task Force was, and continues to be, to develop harmonized systems for the Big Three worldwide. (Even though QS-9000 is not a worldwide industry standard, it is very influential in prescribing automotive requirements for those companies that deal with the Big Three.)

The intent of QS-9000 was to create a requirement for the automotive industry that would meet all the fundamental concepts of quality at the supplier base. However, pressure from the supply base, the registrars, and those who audit to the QS-9000 requirements proved to be somewhat of a challenge in the interpretation of QS-9000 and in how to apply ISO 9000 to QS-9000. As a consequence, the International Automotive Sector Group (IASG) was formed to officially discuss, interpret, and clarify questions, concerns, and issues from suppliers, registrars, and other concerned parties. The agreed-upon interpretations are sanctioned and recognized by the Task Force, the participating ISO 9000 accreditation bodies, and QS-9000 qualified registrars and representatives of the supplier community. The IASG publishes these questions and concerns periodically; the interpretation document can be purchased from ASQC.

The result of the QS-9000 development is that we now have a quality system in the automotive industry that is based on the ISO 9001 structure. It is functional. It can meet international standards. It fulfills the individual requirements of the Big Three automotive companies and, perhaps more importantly, goes beyond the ISO 9000 series where product quality is concerned. A visual representation of QS-9000 is shown in Figure 1.4. The figure represents the four basic ingredients of the QS-9000 requirements, which are ISO 9001, specific customer requirements, industry requirements, and organizational (company) requirements.

In August 1994 these finalized requirements were introduced not only to the automotive companies themselves, but also to their suppliers. The results of this introduction were somewhat bittersweet. On the one hand, everyone through of QS-9000 as "just another program for harmonization" and, on the other hand, some

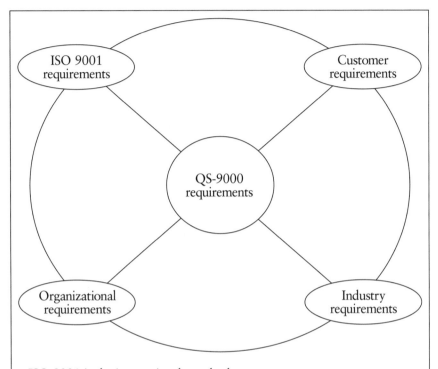

- ISO 9001 is the international standard.
- Customer requirements are Section III of QS-9000.
- Industry requirements are Section II of QS-9000.
- Organizational requirements are a given company's needs, wants, and expectations for a quality system as described in its own documentation in such a way that the other requirements are met.

Note: Some will argue that QS-9000 is a customer requirement in its entirety. However, this figure details the individual components of the QS-9000 requirements.

Figure 1.4. Visualization of the QS-9000 quality system requirements.

suppliers indicated that the requirements were somewhat confusing. To remedy the perception of "just another program" and to clarify the purpose as well as the intent of QS-9000, the Task Force responded with a revision of the QS-9000 requirements effective February 1995. The August 1994 edition was used until January 1996, at which time it became obsolete unless updated with the February 1995 edition. The specific changes introduced in the February 1995 edition were as follows.

- Four updates:
  —Updating the table of contents on page iii
  —Updating GM's registration requirement dates on page 71
  —Updating the method for verifying conformance on page 75
  —Updating the contact person for Ford Motor Co. on page 101

- Four corrections:
  —Correcting the word "assign" to "assignment" in Element 4.1.2.2 (resources) on page 6
  —Correcting the phrase "shall be dependent upon" to "depend upon" in Element 4.2.2 (quality system procedures) on page 10
  —Correcting the phrase "Truck Components" to read "Eaton Truck Components" in the truck manufacturers' specific requirements on page 73
  —Correcting Element 4.2.3 (quality planning) regarding FMEA reference on page 13

- One modification: The customer decision process in Appendix A has been modified for better clarification on page 76. It specifically identifies the quality manual, supporting procedures, self-assessment, and internal audit results as items that may be requested by the customer from the supplier base.

- Three deletions:
  —Deleted the note regarding the accredited laboratories on page 32 dealing with Element 4.10.1 (inspection and testing, general)
  —Deleted two sources in bibliography for Ford Motor Co. on page 68: first, *QOS: Quality Is the Name of the Game* and second, *Supplier Quality Improvement Guidelines for Prototypes*
  —Deleted the two notes from the GM-specific requirements bibliography on page 71

- Fourteen clarifications:
  —Clarify the quality system documentation figure on page 3
  —Clarify Element 4.2.3 (quality planning) regarding the control plan on page 13
  —Clarify the subcontractor development requirements of Element 4.6.2 on page 23
  —Clarify Element 4.9 (process control) regarding government safety and environmental regulations on page 27
  —Clarify Element 4.9 (process control) regarding preventative maintenance on page 28
  —Clarify Element 3.9.2 (preliminary process capability requirements) on page 29
  —Clarify Element 4.9.2 (ongoing process performance requirements) on page 30
  —Clarify Element 4.9.5 (verification of job setups) on page 31
  —Clarify Element 4.12 (inspection and test status) on page 38
  —Clarify Element 4.1.4.2 (correction action) regarding returned product test/analysis on page 42
  —Clarify Element 4.15.6 (delivery) regarding supplier delivery performance monitoring on page 44
  —Clarify Element 4.16 (control of quality records) regarding record retention on page 45

—Clarify the GM-specific requirements regarding layout inspection and functional test on page 72

—Clarify Appendix B, items 2, 3, 5, 10, and 12 regarding code of proactive for quality system registrars on pages 79 and 80

- Thirteen revisions:

—Revise the applicability statement in the introduction section on page 2

—Revise Element 4.1.3 (management review) on page 8

—Revise glossary (regarding accredited laboratory, consulting, control plans, documentation, job instructions, layout inspection, preliminary process capability, procedures, quality manual, subcontractors and suppliers) on pages 94–100

- Eleven additions:

—Add in Element 4.2.3 (quality planning) a note after the prototype for clarification on page 13

—Add in Element 4.5.2 (document and data approval and issue) a note after engineering specifications for further clarification on page 21

—Add in Element 4.7 (control of customer-supplier product) a note for clarification on page 25

—Add in Section II, Element 2.3 (techniques for continuous improvement) two specific methodologies—mistake proofing and analysis of motion/ergonomics—on page 54

—Add under Chrysler-specific requirements the third-party registration requirements on page 58

—Add under Chrysler-specific requirements the lot acceptance sampling table on page 60

—Add under Ford-specific requirements the third-party registration requirements on page 62

—Add under GM-specific requirements the third-party registration requirements on page 70

—Add under GM-specific requirements the document for run rate on page 71

—Add Appendix G clarifying the QS-9000 accreditation body implementation requirements on pages 90–92

—Add Appendix H clarifying the survey audit days, for both an initial audit and ongoing surveillance audit, on page 93

These 50 revisions enhance the QS-9000 substantially, but do not inherently change the focus of the original requirements. They do, however, provide a friendlier, as well as a more understandable, document toward a better quality system in the automotive world.

It is imperative that readers recognize that the QS-9000 document is complex and if there are issues, concerns, or even questions about any of its content, they should contact IASG for further clarification and interpretation at its fax mailbox number, 614-847-8556.

References

Allcock, T., and T. Unsworth. 1991. *Lead auditor course: Training manual.* Detroit: BSI.

Breitenberg, M. 1993. *ISO 9000: Questions and answers on quality, the ISO 9000 standard series, quality system registration, and related issues.* Publication number NISTIR 4721. Gaithersburg, Md.: National Institute of Standards and Technology, U.S. Department of Commerce.

Bureau of Business Practice. 1992. *ISO 9000: Handbook of quality standards and compliance.* Needham Heights, Mass.: Allyn and Bacon.

CEEM Information Services. 1995. *Quality System Update* (January): 1–13.

Corns, M. C. 1968. *The practical operation and management of a bank.* 2nd ed. Boston: Bankers Publishing Company.

Cottman, R. J. 1993. *A guidebook to ISO 9000 and ANSI/ASQC Q90.* Milwaukee, Wis.: ASQC Quality Press.

Crosby, P. 1985. *Quality improvement through defect prevention.* Winter Park, Fla.: Philip Crosby Associates.

Duncan, A. J. 1986. *Quality control and industrial statistics.* 5th ed. Homewood, Ill.: Irwin.

Durant, W. 1954. *Our oriental heritage.* New York: Simon and Schuster.

Goetz, A. 1973. The laws of Eshunnana. In *The ancient near east,* edited by B. Prichard. Vol. 1. Princeton: Princeton University Press.

Guerdan, R. 1956. *Byzantium, its triumphs and tragedy.* New York: George Allen.

Hagigh, S. 1992. Obtaining EC product approvals after 1992: What American manufacturers need to know. *Business America,* 24 February, 20–21.

Johnson, R., and D. Green. 1993. *Lead assessor training.* Singapore: P. E. Batalas.

Kokla, J. W., and G. G. Scott. 1992. *Product liability and product safety directives.* Fairfax, Va.: CEEM Information Services.

Lamprecht, J. L. 1992. *ISO 9000: Preparing for registration.* New York: Marcel Dekker and Milwaukee, Wis.: ASQC Quality Press.

Levy, M. P. 1993. *20 questions and answers on the ISO 9000 standards.* Doc. Q101, rev. 1. Troy, N.Y.: Quality Systems Resource Facility.

Linville, D. 1992. Exporting to the European community. *Business America*, 24 February, 2–3.

MacLean, G. E. 1993. *Documenting quality for ISO 9000 and other industry standards*. Milwaukee, Wis.: ASQC Quality Press.

Meek, T. J. 1973. The code of Hammurabi. In *The ancient near east*, edited by B. Prichard. Vol. 1. Princeton: Princeton University Press.

MIL-Q-9858. 1956. *Quality control system requirements*. Washington, D.C.: Superintendent of Documents.

Morrow, M. 1995. Registrations approach 100,000. *Quality Digest* (January): 25.

Peach, R. W., ed. 1992. *The ISO 9000 handbook*. 2nd ed. Fairfax, Va.: CEEM Information Services.

Stamatis, D. H. 1992. ISO 9000 standards: Are they for real? *ESD Technology* (August): 13–16.

Stamatis, D. H. 1995. *ISO 9000: The basics blocks to quality*. New York: Marcel Dekker.

Trade Adjustment Assistance Centers. 1995. Telephone conversation with author, 9 January.

Voehl, F., P. Jackson, and D. Ashton. 1994. *ISO 9000: An implementation guide for small to mid-sized business*. Delray Beach, Fla.: St. Lucie Press.

CHAPTER 2

Quality Vocabulary

In any field there is a special language specific to the activities of that industry. The ISO world is no different. Most of the definitions that follow are based on ANSI/ISO/ASQC A8402-1994, *Quality Management and Quality Assurance—Vocabulary.* The focus of this chapter is to facilitate an understanding of some of the most common jargon in the ISO series and to offer some commentary on the interpretation of specific words and phrases. Please note that only a selected number of terms and phrases have been identified. For the complete vocabulary see the actual ANSI/ISO/ASQC A8402 standard and the QS-9000 requirements (Chrysler, Ford, and GM 1995), as well as the *IASG Sanctioned QS-9000 Interpretations* (IASG 1995).

This chapter is not intended to explain all the jargon and acronyms used in the automotive industry. Rather, it is meant to make the reader aware of the ANSI/ISO/ASQC point of view regarding these words and short phrases.

Definitions

Concession waiver. Written authorization to use or release a product that does not conform to the specified requirements.

Defect. Nonfulfillment of an intended usage requirement or reasonable expectation, including one concerned with safety.

Design review. Documented, comprehensive, and systematic examination of a design to evaluate its capability to fulfill the requirements for quality, identify problems, if any, and propose the development of solutions.

Grade. Category or rank given to entities having the same functional use but different requirements for quality.

Inspection. Activity such as measuring, examining, testing, or gauging one or more characteristics of an entity and comparing the results with specified requirements in order to establish whether conformity is achieved for each characteristic.

Management review. Formal evaluation by top management of the status and adequacy of the quality system in relation to quality policy and objectives.

Nonconformity. Nonfulfillment of a specified requirement.

Product liability [service liability]. Generic term used to describe the onus on a producer or others to make restitution for loss related to personal injury, property damage, or other harm caused by a product [or service].

Production permit; deviation permit. Written authorization to depart from the originally specified requirements for a product prior to its production.

Quality. Totality of characteristics of an entity that bear on its ability to satisfy stated and implied needs.

Quality assurance. All the planned and systematic activities implemented within the quality system, and demonstrated as needed, to provide adequate confidence that an entity will fulfill requirements for quality.

Quality audit. Systematic and independent examination to determine whether quality activities and related results comply with planned arrangements and whether these arrangements are implemented effectively and are suitable to achieve objectives.

Quality control. Operating techniques and activities that are used to fulfill requirements for quality.

Quality loop. Conceptual model of interacting activities that influence quality at the various stages ranging from the identification of needs to the assessment of whether these needs have been satisfied. Note—The *quality spiral* is a similar concept.

Quality management. All activities of the overall management function that determine the quality policy, objectives, and responsibilities, and implement them by means such as quality planning, quality control, quality assurance, and quality improvement within the quality system.

Quality plan. Document setting out the specific quality practices, resources, and sequence of activities relevant to a particular product, project, or contract.

Quality policy. Overall intentions and direction of an organization with regard to quality, as formally expressed by top management.

Quality surveillance. Continual monitoring and verification of the status of an entity, and analysis of records to ensure that specified requirements are being fulfilled.

Quality system. Organizational structure, procedures, processes, and resources needed to implement quality management.

Reliability. The ability of an item to perform to a required quality standard over time.

Specification. Document stating requirements.

Traceability. Ability to trace the history, application, or location of an entity by means of recorded identifications.

Comments

The following comments on the definitions just given are offered for further explanation and/or clarification of the specific terms. They are offered in the spirit of making the ISO standards friendlier and easier to understand. They are not by any means to be used instead of the actual word and/or definition as provided in ANSI/ISO/ASQC A8402 or by another source.

Furthermore, if there is a specific concern about the meaning of a specific element of QS-9000, the reader is strongly encouraged to obtain the most recent copy of the *IASG Sanctioned QS-9000 Interpretations*. A copy may be purchased by calling ASQC at 800-248-1946.

Quality

1. The term *quality* is not used to express a degree of excellence in a comparative sense nor is it used in a quantitative sense for technical evaluations. When it is necessary to identify the quality in these terms, the specific and appropriate adjective should be used. For example,

> *Relative quality* should be used where products or services are ranked on a relative basis—by the degree of excellence or some comparative sense.

> *Quality level* and *quality measure* should be used where precise technical evaluations are carried out in a quantitative sense.

2. In a contractual environment needs are specified. In other environments, implied needs should be identified and defined where appropriate.

3. Where possible, the needs (specifications/requirements), wants, and expectations of the customer ought to be identified and defined.

4. We must recognize that our needs can change over time. This implies the periodic revision of requirements. Generally, the flow of change is as follows:

> Needs become obsolete.

> Wants become needs.

> Expectations become wants.

> Other expectations become expectations.

> The cycle repeats.

5. Needs are usually translated into features and characteristics with specified criteria based on the specific customer. These needs may include, but are not limited to, aspects of usability, safety, availability, economics, environment, reliability, and maintainability.

6. Product and service quality are always influenced by many stages of interactive activities (negotiation) and optimization of related activities, such as design, production, service operation, maintenance, finance, and so on.

7. The economic achievement of satisfactory quality involves all stages of the quality loop. If some stages are identified, it is only for emphasis. For example, quality attributable to design or quality attributable to service or quality attributable to implementation or quality attributable to production, and so on.

8. Remember that quality is defined by the customer. Unless the needs, wants, and expectations of the customer are satisfied or exceeded, there is no quality. Some other definitions may be appropriate, such as *fitness for use* (the Juran traditional definition), *price of conformance/nonconformance* (the Crosby definition), *continual improvement* (the Deming definition), and so on. These all represent some facet of quality, and in all cases a fuller explanation is required. While differences must be recognized, the emphasis of quality is—or ought to be—on the functional use/cost (value) relationship.

Grade

1. Grade always reflects a planned and/or recognized difference in requirements. The emphasis is on use/cost relationship.

2. Where grade is identified numerically, it is common for the highest grade to be 1 and the lower grades to be 2, 3, and so on. If the grade is identified by a point score or a pictogram, then the lowest grade usually has the fewest points or pictures, respectively.

3. We must remember that a high-grade product or service may be of inadequate quality as far as satisfying the needs of the customer.

Quality policy

1. The quality policy is only one element of the corporate policy and is authorized only by top management.

Quality management

1. Quality management includes strategic planning, allocation of resources, and other systematic activities for quality such as quality planning, operations, and evaluations.

2. The responsibility for quality management always belongs to top management. This is contrasted with the attainment of desired quality, which requires the commitment and participation of all members of the organization.

Quality assurance

1. Quality assurance within an organization serves as a management tool. On the other hand, in contractual situations, quality assurance also serves to provide confidence to the customer. In order to provide confidence, it may be necessary to produce evidence of effectiveness.

2. Quality assurance requires continual evaluation of factors that affect the adequacy of the design, specification, verification, and audits of production, installation, and inspection operations.

3. Quality assurance is complete only when the requirements reflect the needs, wants, and expectations of the user.

4. Quality assurance always focuses on and emphasizes the *planning* of quality as opposed to the *appraisal* of quality. Planning looks at the system of quality from a prevention point of view. Appraisal, on the other hand, looks at the product quality from a sorting point of view.

Quality control

1. Quality control involves operational techniques and activities aimed both at monitoring a process and at eliminating root causes of unsatisfactory performance at relevant stages of the quality loop. The ultimate goal is economic effectiveness.

2. When referring to quality control, special care should be taken in describing what really is meant, so that confusion is avoided. For example, is manufacturing quality control the same as company-wide quality control?

3. Quality control focuses on and emphasizes the *appraisal* of quality as opposed to the *planning* of quality.

Quality system

1. Some of the most important issues in any quality system are the complexity, length, comprehensiveness, and so on. The quality system should only be as complex, comprehensive, and so on as needed (appropriate and adequate) to meet the quality objectives.

2. Remember that the objectives are defined by the organization. So, in the quality system, the organization tells the world what it is going to do.

3. In contractual situations, demonstration of the implementation of your quality system and its elements may be required. (For ISO certification, the demonstration is a must and is conducted by a third-party assessor.)

Quality audit

1. While the quality system tells the world what the organization is going to do, the audit makes sure that the organization has fulfilled its promises. Quality system audits are performed for ISO certification.

2. To maintain the integrity of the system, the audit must be conducted by staff not directly responsible for the areas being audited.

3. Quality audits can be conducted for internal or external purposes.

4. Audits have many purposes, including, but not limited to, management information, corrective action, benchmarking the organization for future evaluation on improvement, and so on.

5. Under no circumstances should a quality audit be confused with or used in lieu of surveillance or inspection activities, which are performed for the sole purpose of process control or product acceptance.

Quality surveillance

1. Quality surveillance may be carried out by or on behalf of the customer to ensure that the contractual requirements are being met.

2. Surveillance may have to take into account factors that can result in deterioration or degradation with time.

3. For ISO certification, surveillance by the registrar is mandatory and is performed either once or twice a year, depending on the registrar. The registrar also has the right to come into the organization at any time, with or without notice. The QS-9000 document requires a surveillance every six months.

Design review

1. Design reviews by themselves do not ensure proper design.

2. A design review may be conducted at any stage of the design process.

3. The participants at each design review must be qualified for all functions affecting the design at hand and quality of the product.

4. The focus of the design review will depend on the objective and scope of the product. Generally, some of the most common items reviewed are

Capability of the design

    Fitness for purpose

    Feasibility

    Manufacturability

    Measurability

    Performance

    Reliability

    Maintainability

    Safety

    Environmental aspects

    Life-cycle costs

Monitoring (reviewing) the design

Traceability

1. The term *traceability* has at least three main meanings.

   • In a distribution sense, it relates to a product or service.

   • In a calibration sense, it relates measuring equipment to some standard (physical constant(s), properties; national; international).

   • In a data collection sense, it relates calculations and data generated throughout the quality loop to a product or service.

2. Traceability requirements should be as specific as possible for some stated period of time and point of origin.

Change waiver or letter of deviations

1. Waivers should specify limited quantities, periods, or specified uses.

2. All waivers should be signed by the appropriate authorized person.

Reliability

1. Sometimes the term *reliability* is used to denote a probability of success or a success ratio.

2. The field of reliability is always reviewed. Thus, the definition may change (see IEC Publication 271 for updates).

Product liability

1. Of utmost importance is the fact that the limits on liability vary from country to country according to national legislation.

2. The European Union is in the process of developing a series of product liability directives. As the directives are developed and implemented, the world of product liability will be somewhat standardized.

Nonconformity

1. The definition of *nonconformity* covers the absence and/or departure of one or more quality characteristics or quality system elements from specified requirements (compare with note 1 under Defect).

Defect

1. The definition of *defect* covers the absence and/or departure of one or more quality characteristics from intended usage requirements (compare with note 1 under Nonconformity).

2. Of special interest here is the fact that legal requirements and consequences from the use of the word *defect* can be extremely

costly for an organization. Therefore, whenever possible, avoid the word *defect* and use the word *nonconforming.*

Specification

1. A specification should refer to or include drawings and all relevant documents. In addition, the specification should also indicate the means and the criteria whereby conformity can be verified.

References

ANSI/ISO/ASQC. 1994. ANSI/ISO/ASQC A8402-1994, *Quality management and quality assurance—Vocabulary.* Milwaukee, Wis.: ASQC.

Chrysler Corporation, Ford Motor Company, and General Motors Corporation. 1995. *Quality system requirements: QS-9000.* Southfield, Mich.: Chrysler Corporation, Ford Motor Company, and General Motors Corporation.

International Automotive Sector Group. 1995. *IASG sanctioned QS-9000 interpretations,* 28 September. N.p.: International Automotive Sector Group, fax mailbox number 614-847-8556.

CHAPTER 3

Quality System Requirements

There are many tools and techniques to improve process controls and a whole series of approaches to teamwork and improvement issues. The family of ISO 9000 standards helps to provide the infrastructure for the systems side of total quality management (TQM) and, in more general terms, a system of quality. This chapter addresses the intent of ISO 9001 and provides a meaningful and detailed interpretation. The focus here will be the management responsibilities covered in ISO 9001. For companywide activities, see Chapter 6. For the QS-9000 requirements, see Chapter 4.

Overview
ANSI/ISO/ASQC A8402-1994 defines *quality assurance* as

> *All the planned and systematic activities implemented within the quality system, and demonstrated as needed, to provide adequate confidence that an entity will fulfill requirements for quality.*

This definition, then, requires the purchaser (the company; the user) to have a set of rules giving confidence that when a product and/or service is purchased from a supplier it will consistently meet the purchaser's needs. This set of rules is applied to a supplier to give assurance that its systems work. This system is driven to the subcontractor base with the expectation and confidence that quality will be controlled and optimized at all levels. This push is expressed in Figure 3.1.

One of the most serious issues, then, is the question of how to manage quality. Note that the emphasis is on management, not control. Figure 3.1 demonstrates that the quality confidence is only as good as the incoming quality from the suppliers and their subcontractors. Furthermore, for that quality to exist, it must be defined. Management is in control of that definition.

In deciding on the method of application of ISO 9000 to a company, it is important for the organization to (1) consider the specific requirements placed on the organization related to regulated industries, and (2) understand the specific jargon of the standards.

1. A regulated industry is an industry that produces products for which the EU Commission has developed or is developing an EU-wide technical harmonization directive. These directives provide

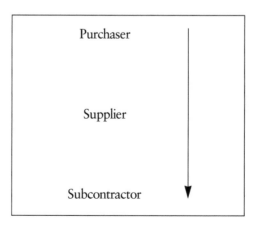

Figure 3.1. Confidence in suppliers.

manufacturers with a single set of requirements for products offered for sale in the EU. Currently, a partial list of the directives includes

Toys

Simple pressure devices

Personal protection equipment

Gas appliances

Product conformity testing

Construction products

Machines

Medical devices

Telecommunication terminal equipment

The specific industries addressed by these directives must follow basic quality system requirements and, in some cases, additional requirements. For example, the FDA and software, automotive, nuclear, and other industries may use ISO 9000 as a framework for their quality system. However, additional specific requirements may be necessary to comply with the regulated industries.

In the case of the automotive industry, ISO 9001 serves as the framework of the quality system. To that base, additional customer-specific requirements have been added. The combination of these specific requirements and ISO 9001 is *Quality System Requirements: QS-9000*. Guidelines on these specific requirements are in development and they are updated on a continual basis.

2. Understanding a standard's use of jargon will facilitate implementation. Of special interest are the following words.

- *May*—The word *may* implies the things that would give the quality system developer benefits if incorporated in the documentation. These elements are optional.

- *Should*—When the standard uses the word *should,* it implies the things that are specifically recommended by an industry and are important to an effective quality system.

- *Shall*—When the standard addresses something with *shall,* it implies the things that the organization is required to define and carry out. It may be directed to a specific standard or document.

Key Features of the ISO 9000 Series

The ISO 9000 series consists of five documents—ISO 9000-1, ISO 9001, ISO 9002, ISO 9003, ISO 9004-1. Specifically,

- ISO 9000-1 is a set of quality guidelines for selection and use of quality management and quality assurance standards.

- The ISO 9001 quality system is a model for quality assurance in design, development, production, installation, and servicing.

- The ISO 9002 quality system is a model for quality assurance in production, installation, and servicing.

- The ISO 9003 quality system is a model for quality assurance in final inspection and test.

- The ISO 9004-1 quality management and quality system elements provide guidelines for developing a quality system under which a company could seek registration to ISO 9001, 9002, or 9003.

ISO 9001, ISO 9002, and ISO 9003 are system requirement standards written in mandatory language, which allows the documents to be used in contract conditions. As a consequence, these are the only standards that a given organization may consider for certification. On the other hand, ISO 9000-1 and ISO 9004-1 are written as guidelines to select the appropriate system and to define the elements that the system should cover, respectively.

The use of numbers does not indicate differing degrees of excellence. That is, ISO 9001 certification is not better than ISO 9002, which, in turn, is not better than ISO 9003. They are system requirements for specific applications. When a company undertakes innovative design and its customers are likely to require assurance of design capability, then it must inevitably operate to ISO 9001. However, if a company produces products against established specifications or provides a service against a written requirement for service delivery, then ISO 9002 may be adequate to meet those needs.

The emphasis of the international standards is on the management of quality systems. While all the clauses of the standards are relevant and important to the company's effective operation, there are certain key features that highlight the strength of the document in terms of correcting the causes of problems and improving inputs to ensure that outputs are meeting expectations.

When one considers the requirements of ISO 9001, it is useful to think in three distinct areas.

1. Management responsibilities

2. Companywide activities

3. Specific requirements

On the other hand, when one works with QS-9000, it is useful to consider the following approach.

1. The basic ISO 9001 requirements

2. The sector-specific requirements

3. The customer-specific requirements

Note that while QS-9000 has as its base the traditional approach (ISO 9001), the last two categories provide additional requirements. The sector-specific requirements are items that can be audited by a third-party auditor during the certification process—just like the basic ISO items. The customer-specific requirements are audited by the customer through a second-party audit. In this situation, the organization must conform to the specific requirements in order for the certification to be issued. The Automotive Task Force has developed a guide for such an audit, called the *Quality System Assessment* (Chrysler, Ford, and GM 1994). It may be purchased from the office of AIAG.

Review of ISO 9001, Section 4—Management Responsibilities

Section 4 is the actual certifiable portion of the standard. What follows is a detailed explanation and interpretation on a per-element (clause-by-clause) basis.

Clause 4.1. Management responsibility. Clause 4.1 is extensive, consisting of five subsections, each of which highlights particular activities that senior management must undertake. It is significant that this first clause in the certifiable portion of the standard demands that senior management organize and plan for quality. In other words, the quality responsibility cannot be delegated to the lower levels of management. Senior management is always responsible for, and must be dedicated to, quality. Senior management's commitment to quality must be exemplary; being involved is not enough. Lack of upper management commitment to the quality program results in the allocation of important resources to other programs.

As part of this dedication and commitment, senior management must always reinforce with words and deeds what quality is and what it means to the organization. It is senior management's responsibility to advocate improvement and consistency. In addition, senior management should ask for and review proof of documented improvements (see also 4.17).

Clause 4.1.1. Quality policy. Before anyone in any company can hope to be consistent in any activity, there must be a policy. In this policy, objectives must be enumerated so that the policy becomes an instrument of direction and vision for the company.

It is not enough to say "This is our policy" or "These are our objectives." They must be documented. Documentation implies collaboration between any two sources (for example, individuals, reports, procedures). It is of paramount importance to recognize that the ISO 9001 standard does require documentation and maintenance of a quality system (see 4.2.1 and 4.2.2). Because of this requirement the written form of documentation becomes the most expedient and accurate for the system.

Specifically, clause 4.1.1 requires a company to define and document its objectives as well as its policy for quality. Objectives are the quantified goals that are specified and then attained. Knowing the destination (goal) allows managers to plan the journey to quality. Because this commitment to documentation is important and necessary, management must find a way to tell everyone in the organization what the policy and objectives are and how they affect people individually and collectively. This means finding a way to cascade the understanding of the quality system down the levels of the organization, at each level making sure that the system has been installed and that provisions for its maintenance have been accounted for.

While the policy is formulated by the most senior group of managers, company objectives for quality will require the participation of many managers, as their efforts influence these objectives. There are some benefits to this extended participation.

- The act of defining helps to unify managers.

- Involvement of the managers is necessary to operating on a planned basis rather than from crisis to crisis or department to department.

- This method enables a subsequent comparison of performance against objectives.

Objectives in quality may be a reduction in scrap, complaints, rework, returns, and so on. Or, the objectives may be merely to define a certain performance. In order to make the system improve, the objectives chosen should be those that will improve some aspect of the company's performance, delivery, lead time, response, reliability, and so on.

Clause 4.1.2. Organization

Clause 4.1.2.1. Responsibility and authority. Clause 4.1.2.1. is concerned with making sure that the various tasks in an organization are clearly defined, and people's authority to manage, perform, or check work is also clearly defined. This definition of authority should be traceable to senior management.

Having defined and agreed upon the quality policy and objectives in writing, the way is cleared for the next stage of the process. This is often accomplished by preparing schematic organization charts showing technical and functional interfaces and may include job descriptions for the positions shown on the chart, if the company wishes to use that method. It is strongly recommended that in the organizational chart, positions should be listed as opposed to names. The reason for this is that people move more frequently than the organization changes. As a consequence, fewer changes will be required.

The detail is based on necessity. It has to be clear to outsiders that the organization is defined. To insiders it must be clear exactly what constitutes each person's job and the limits of his or her authority and responsibility. Furthermore, it must demonstrate the relationship of the quality authority as it relates to senior management.

The actions and decisions made here will cover the requirement in the standard relating to responsibility and authority (4.1.2.1). If your organization operates under a business unit or matrix structure, make sure that the responsibility and authority for quality are visible and effective. Make sure that there is no conflicting responsibility.

Clause 4.1.2.2. Resources. An important feature of any control activity is the objectivity of the verification and the independence of the person verifying. The bias of any impropriety must be eliminated. Doubt of objectivity must be removed. The standard requires that management examine what work is being done and ensure that, where necessary, there is a means of verifying that it has been done the way management expected. Furthermore, this clause requires that appropriate training must be in place to facilitate the assigned work task(s).

Clause 4.1.2.3. Management representative. The senior management must appoint someone as a representative to ensure that the standard is being followed and to assist in its implementation and effectiveness. It does not matter what other duties this person may have as long as he or she is in a position with the defined authority and responsibility. There must be a direct link or traceability to senior management.

Quite often, the management representative position is filled by the quality manager; but anyone appointed by the senior management and given the authority and responsibility can provide this function. When that happens, this management representative is called the ISO 9000 facilitator, the ISO 9000 coordinator, or the ISO management representative. This facilitator (or whatever the person is called) may or may not be a full-time employee. The purpose, duties, and/or functions of this facilitator may cover several diverse activities. Some of the diverse activities are

- Internal audits
- Inspection
- Statistical methods
- Quality/inspection planning

- Corrective action
- Product liability
- Calibration
- Supplier certification or surveillance

- Defect prevention programs
- Customer complaints analyses
- Monitoring the improvement
- Quality costs
- Training
- Implementation process

- Helping in the selection of consultant(s)
- Communicating progress to management
- Coaching the implementation teams
- Direct appropriate and applicable course(s) of action

The list is not meant to be exhaustive. Neither is the list mandatory. It merely gives some examples of traditional duties associated with the function of the ISO facilitator (the management representative).

Clause 4.1.3. Management review. Once the system is installed, management is responsible for reviewing its effectiveness and appropriateness. It must be remembered that the system belongs to management because management has the responsibility to define it and generate the policy of operation and objectives, which, all together, helped establish the system. It is of paramount importance that this review take place at specific intervals because without it the quality system will stagnate.

The review may take either a formal or informal format as long as critical information is reviewed and the process is documented. Management reviews generally include, but are not limited to, the following activities:

- Assessment of the internal audit results
- Review of corrective actions
- Review of suggested changes
- System monitoring

Clause 4.2. Quality system. Clause 4.2 requires management to formally define the activities necessary in more detailed documents. Typical documents are procedures, instructions, and standard operating procedures (SOPs). The reason for the detail is to put this documentation into practice and to make sure that the processes are working effectively.

Of special interest is the expression *specified requirements.* It is used for the first time in the standard and it means any requirements an organization is required to fulfill.

- Contract requirements specified by a customer in a contract and agreed to by the supplier

- The policy, objectives, procedures, and instructions that the management defines for use within the company

- The quality management system standard (that is, ISO 9001, ISO 9002, or ISO 9003)

- Regulatory requirements

- Directives in product or service lines

In addition to these specific items, the clause also requires quality system procedures (4.2.2) and quality planning (4.2.3). The detail for both of these clauses will depend on the complexity of the work, the methods used, and the skills and training needed by the personnel involved in carrying out the activity.

Clause 4.3. Contract review. In order for a supplier to meet customers' requirements, the supplier must know what those requirements are and know that they can be met when the order is taken. This means reviewing each order and providing a record of the review.

When two parties undertake a contract, each must understand clearly and agree upon what is to be supplied. Only by reviewing all the contract requirements fully can a company be sure that it will satisfy its customer.

The key steps in contract review are as follows.

- Ensure that the requirements are clearly understood and agreed upon by both parties and that these requirements are recorded and kept.

- Review all the requirements internally to ensure that the resources, organization, and facilities are available and capable of meeting all technical and commercial requirements.

- Review any subsequent changes to determine their effect on meeting the requirements.

Although the standard is written around the situation involving a tender document (a response to a request for a quote or a bid) typical of a large project, the principles are as true where purchase is made of a simple catalog item. The reader should notice that the definition of a tender used in the previous sentence is somewhat different from the definition used in the ISO 9000 series, which defines *tender* as an offer made by a supplier in response to an invitation to satisfy a contract award to provide product. Someone has to ensure that the customer's requirements of item, delivery, and so on can be met.

It is not always recognized that the content of sales literature that is sent out to many customers constitutes a contract when purchase is made on the basis of those claims. ISO 9001 can have the very desirable effect of causing such literature to state what can be done as opposed to what we would like to be done.

Many of today's companies utilize a checklist in the order entry system that requires certain items of information to be supplied before the order can be processed. While this is relatively easy on a computer system, manual methods for defining the specification in this way can be very effective as well.

The clause is further developed to include reviews that must be defined and documented (4.3.2) and information on how to handle amendments to the contract (4.3.3) and how to maintain appropriate records (4.3.4).

Clause 4.4. Design control. To think that a single clause in a standard would adequately cover all the requirements of design control is presumptuous. This clause identifies the minimum requirements of design control that a company has to define formally and how it should comply with these requirements. The complexity of this clause is demonstrated by the six main subdivisions, some of which are further divided to define specific requirements of design.

Clause 4.4.1. General. The general requirement is for a method of controlling the design activity and verifying that the design meets the requirements. The requirements may be customer specific, industry specific, and/or regulation specific.

The rest of the subclauses specifically address the requirements of sound design.

Clause 4.4.2. Design and development planning. Planning is essential to quality in any task. This clause demands that a plan—perhaps in the form of advanced quality planning, control plans, feasibility reviews, quality function deployment (QFD), a block diagram, reliability calculations, failure mode and effects analysis (FMEA), or design reviews—has to be prepared that references the responsibility for doing and the responsibility for verifying at each stage. As the design evolves, the plan will need to change to reflect the changes in the design. The plan, therefore, becomes dynamic— always ready to accommodate the changed design.

Furthermore, this plan must cover the concerns of how the company will keep up-to-date in both design and development. The plan must be descriptive, as it has to communicate to someone who is not familiar with the design. At least one way of handling this situation is to have a procedure and instructions covering the specifics of the design.

The responsibilities for each part of the design must be specified. The parts may be in the form of (a) system, (b) subassembly, or (c) component.

Clause 4.4.3. Organizational and technical interfaces. The essence of this clause is to ensure that the inputs for the design are cross-functional and multidisciplined in nature. The standard recognizes that no designer works alone. What that implies is that for the design to be its best, other departments—that is, production, sales, purchasing, servicing, inspection, and others—must have input to that design. Information, therefore, needs to be concise, relevant, and current, so that the status can be established at any point in time. In this way, valid design decisions are made more easily.

The standard is concerned with the means of ensuring that information necessary to different groups is properly and adequately received and reviewed. Therefore, the mechanism for controlling that information is important and needs formal definition by management.

The people involved in the design work have to be qualified. That does not mean that everyone has to have a journeyman's card or a college degree. Rather, it means that management has to decide what qualifications, experiences, and training are appropriate and adequate for the designated task.

All design personnel should have the appropriate credentials and certifications for their respective tasks. These should be properly documented with the design department and/or the human resources department. The definition for the credentials and certifications may be found in a job specification, job description, or personnel records. In some cases, these requirements may be found in procedures or department guidelines. The actual location of these sources will depend on the organization.

In essence, this clause emphasizes the need for identification as to who does what, who is responsible for verifying each part of the design, what are the qualifications of personnel, how to define the qualifications, how the qualifications were formalized, and how to keep them current.

Clause 4.4.4. Design input. All inputs necessary to a design have to be identified, reviewed by authorized persons for validity, and documented. The keys steps here are *identification, selection,* and *documentation.*

The specificity of the standard requires appropriate documentation and review. To prove that a system exists, appropriate documentation must exist. Minutes of meetings, memos, design reviews, and other pertinent data do qualify as appropriate; however, they must be kept and updated as needed. The review of these documents must establish that incomplete or ambiguous requirements are resolved between all input sources and the designer(s).

Clause 4.4.5. Design output. The design function produces something that can be made and tested and that complies with what the customer requested. Design output may be in the form of drawings, calculations, specifications, analyses, and so on. These should refer to the design inputs, which determined the requirements, and also state or refer to the acceptance criteria (that is, what defines that this product will be correct?).

Within the specification, all requirements must be addressed (legal, regulatory, customer, and any part of the design that is crucial to the safety and proper functioning of the product).

The design has to be finished at some point and be deemed complete. At that point the design output documents must be reviewed before the release date. The completion point must be identified and stated in the form of the media required, product features, calculations and analysis, and so on. That basis must relate directly to input, conform with the appropriate regulatory requirements, and identify characteristics that relate to safe and proper functioning of the product.

Clause 4.4.6. Design review. Clause 4.4.6 emphatically requires design reviews at appropriate stages of the design process. There is no list in the standard to define what is appropriate—the standard provides leeway for each organization to comply with this clause. It certainly implies that cross-functional and multidisciplined teams are appropriate. Furthermore, it suggests that a company has freedom to define its own design verification in addition to regulatory and customer requirements. Some examples of design verification include design reviews, alternative calculations, and comparisons with similar proven designs.

Clause 4.4.7. Design verification. A means of verifying the design must be defined. There is no specific list in the standard to define what is appropriate. However, the standard provides under note 10 a recommendation of some of the activities that may be used, including design reviews, alternative calculations, comparisons with similar proven designs, reviewing the design stage, and undertaking tests and demonstrations.

Checking or verifying the design must take place against the requirements agreed upon at the start and as the design evolves. Some companies do this by a series of design reviews within the project team, with occasional attendance by external people. A design review, occurring at various stages or milestones during the design project, may include the following criteria, among others.

- Reliability
- Maintainability
- Inspectability
- Durability

Other companies may utilize computer-aided design (CAD) systems, simulations, prototypes, or technical audits by qualified persons independent of the design.

As part of the verification process, others may use alternative methods of calculations (reliability engineering), testing, FMEA, or any other available tool that is appropriate for the particular design.

Many designs are modifications of previous designs—designs that in the past have demonstrated a capability of performance. Where these designs utilize common principles, the existing data can be used as acceptable for verification.

Whatever the method used, the complete process of verification must be a formal one.

Clause 4.4.8. Design validation. The standard provides a short list—under notes—of where validation is appropriate. The list is meant as a guideline, not a prescriptive approach to validation. What the clause establishes is the need for such an activity, with appropriate documentation.

Clause 4.4.9. Design change. The changes made to the design must be clear and documented. In addition, changes must show a level of review consistent with the original preparation of the various parts of the design (that is, the same authority).

Any design is likely to change before it is complete. Before permitting change, the following types of questions need to be addressed.

- Does the product still conform to the original requirements?
- Is its fitness for use affected?
- Can it still be made, tested, and so on?
- Will it affect safety or operation?
- Is there anything else that would be affected?

Clause 4.5. Document control

Clause 4.5.1. General. Clause 4.5.1 establishes the need for documented procedures to control all documents and data that relate to the requirements.

Clause 4.5.2. Document and data approval and issue. Documentation and paperwork generally are not in short supply in most companies. What is usually not available is the correct documentation (appropriate, adequate, up-to-date, with the obsolete documentation properly removed, approved by the right person or persons).

One of the most common areas of deficiency in quality assurance systems is the control of documents. The focus of document control is to ensure that the right version or issue of the document is available. To facilitate this, a document distribution list should exist to allow all current holders of a document to receive updates.

The standard implies that only authorized documents should be in use. Therefore, a system of approval should be stated. In reality, however, it is sometimes necessary to refer to out-of-date specifications or complete sets of obsolete documentation. This is acceptable as long as it is clear on the document or in reference documents that it is out-of-date.

All organizations have the need for temporary changes, perhaps allowing certain authorized persons to make handwritten changes to a document. This is acceptable as long as changes are made according to a defined and authorized procedure and the persons affected are aware.

Any document (drawings, procedures, instructions) that experiences a great deal of change will ultimately need to be amended or completely revised. There can be no set rule for this, but if there is a danger of confusion because of multiple changes, the document needs to be reissued.

Clause 4.5.3. Document and data changes. Documentation needing change must be changed, provided the change goes through the same authority that approved the original document. When a document is changed, persons using the document must be able to find out what the change was.

Clause 4.6. Purchasing

Clause 4.6.1. General. The requirement for clause 4.6.1 is to identify that the company placing an order from a supplier or subsupplier is responsible for ensuring that whatever is bought is correct. What this implies is that the company must have in place systems that ensure the conformance of the product and/or service purchased based on the requirements that are set forth in the contract to purchase.

Clause 4.6.2. Evaluation of subcontractors. The standard requires that the company actively considers the reasons for choice of a subcontractor and can show evidence of the reason for the choice. The decision must be based on what the buying company considers important. The requirements here demand that a sound basis be established for the use of subcontractors and that the information given to them is clear.

The basis for selection may be by various means. It may be that as a policy the company wishes to use only suppliers who have been assessed and certified by an accredited third party. This policy may, of course, limit the choice of suppliers. However, the company may require it as a condition for doing business and may insist that, within a given time, all its suppliers must gain certification. This kind of policy has been at least one of the reasons for the growth of registration.

Other bases for selection of a supplier may include any one or combination of the following: an assessment by the company itself, assessment by a regulatory agency, assessment by a specific contractual agreement of the customer, or a product assessment. The criteria for the selection should be established by the company, taking into account the degree of assurance necessary from that supplier.

History of satisfactory supply from a supplier can provide the evidence necessary for acceptance. Such an assessment may be the result of incoming product inspection, delivery performance, after-sales service received, response time to complaints, corrective action, follow-up, and so on.

In the absence of registered suppliers through third-party registration, the company is required to have a formal certification program that identifies the suppliers in a tier system such as the following.

1. *Certified.* The certified level constitutes the most advanced self-certification. Most purchases are done with this kind of supplier. The relationship is looked upon as a win–win situation.

2. *Preferred.* Preferred status is lower than certified. The supplier has the potential of becoming a certified supplier if it follows the quality systems prescribed by the customer.

3. *Approved.* Approved suppliers are without historical data. Usually, minimal interaction takes place with these suppliers.

Depending on the certification level attained by the supplier, the company may accept the product and/or service from the supplier based on a monitoring program. The monitoring will make sure that the criteria established as being important are followed and meet the requirements. The monitoring may be implemented through statistical process control (SPC), incoming inspection, and other statistical formats.

Clause 4.6.3. Purchasing data. One of the most explicit requirements in the standard is clause 4.6.3. It requires absolutely full and clear detail on the purchasing document.

The information sent to the supplier as an order should be considered as external work instructions. Orders and supplements should be under approved document control and should describe exactly what is necessary in order for the supplier to comply.

The requirements for the content of a purchase order can be specified as a procedure. Also, addressed in this clause is the requirement of review and approval of purchasing documents—which, of course, become records—for adequacy.

Clause 4.6.4. Verification of purchased product. Clause 4.6.4 is subdivided into 4.6.4.1 and 4.6.4.2. The essence of both clauses is the concern of companies accustomed to visits by customer representatives to the suppliers or the company. It must be clear that when a customer inspects the product, the company is not absolved from its responsibility for purchasing the correct product.

During purchase from a supplier, it may be that the company's customer wishes to verify at the supplier's or company's facilities that the products purchased comply. If this is an important condition to the company, then a clause in the purchasing agreement may be necessary to formalize this right.

Regardless of who executes the purchase and how it is verified, neither the company nor the customer nor the supplier is absolved from their obligations under the contract between them.

Clause 4.7. Control of customer-supplied product. Where a customer supplies material or product to be incorporated into the final product by the supplier, the supplier must ensure that the material is correct and is stored and handled correctly. A company must have a way of dealing with such situations. The best way is to include the checking, handling, storage, and so on of this material under the control system for its own supplied product.

Clause 4.8. Product identification and traceability. The product identification and traceability requirement is particularly flexible to encourage the principle of adding unique identities to the product to tie it to specifications, drawings, and so on. The degree of traceability necessary, or even possible, varies greatly across different industries.

In safety-oriented and critical industries, traceability back to the original source is maintained by unique identity numbers on the product itself. Lesser requirements may indicate traceability back to purchase location only, or, in the case of certain products—textiles, for example—the country of origin. The necessity for recall of a product will determine the extent of traceability.

During manufacturing, identification is often attained by accompanying documents by batch, lot, or any other appropriate means of identification.

Clause 4.9. Process control. The process control requirement deals with production installation and servicing processes that directly affect quality. The control requirement may include aspects of process approval by qualification and monitoring. Whatever method is used, it must be clear exactly what constitutes success.

This clause explains the manufacturing function and contains one of the most contentious statements in the standard. The requirement states the need to formally plan the stages of production necessary and, furthermore, it requires the processes to be "carried out under controlled conditions [including] documented work instruction defining the manner of production and installation where the absence of such instructions would adversely affect quality."

The requirement is that written instructions are necessary everywhere—except where they are not needed. Only management can decide where an instruction must be formal.

It must be made clear to all personnel in the organization what it is that they are required to do. The written word is perhaps the most common, efficient, and objective way of transmitting this information.

Some of the reasons for making a procedure formal are as follows.

1. If it is a specified requirement (that is, part of a contract), a requirement by the manager of the department, or a requirement of the quality systems standard, then it must be formal.

2. If there is a difference of opinion between the manager who is responsible and the staff who have to operate the procedure, then a written procedure may help to overcome that difference.

3. Where inputs to a procedure are made by different people, perhaps in different departments, a written procedure may help in ensuring a common understanding.

4. Where it is necessary historically to understand the basis for records, a written procedure can help to provide the information.

5. If it is necessary to bring in people who do not usually operate that procedure, a written procedure can help.

6. Whenever an employee unofficially (for his or her own benefit only) makes a written record of a process, there is an established need for a written procedure. In this case, there is a high likelihood that formal written procedures will be created.

The implication of these statements is that management must demand that appropriate education and training be available and must encourage the involved employees to participate. Once the training has been established and implemented, management must provide a system to monitor and evaluate the effectiveness of employees' implementation of their training.

Further requirements within this clause allow the company to consider the use of various process controls or checking of product features to maintain control and, in all cases, to provide people with a clear specification of success (a written standard, a picture, a representative sample, and so on).

The scope of 4.9 includes processes that cannot be fully verified by inspection, testing, and so on. In these processes, deficiencies will be apparent only after the product is in use. Under these conditions, the processes must be carried out under strict documentation with appropriate equipment and qualified operator(s).

Certain processes, by their nature, can only be controlled by predefined requirements being followed by personnel qualified in some particular skill. Inspection of the finished product would not be effective in determining whether there are deficiencies. Such processes require a degree of prequalification and strict monitoring against prescribed procedures. Examples include welding, forging, casting, soldering, plastic molding, certain food and drug manufacturing, software coding, and heat treating.

Clause 4.10. Inspection and testing

Clause 4.10.1. General. Clause 4.10.1 defines the necessity for establishing and maintaining documented procedures for inspection and testing activities to verify conformance to the requirements.

Clause 4.10.2. Receiving inspection and testing. Clause 4.10.2 is subdivided into three categories (4.10.2.1, 4.10.2.2, and 4.10.2.3). In all three categories the emphasis is on items purchased from suppliers and the state of incoming quality. If there are problems with the incoming quality, the product must not be used unless the problems are corrected. The incoming product must meet the contractual requirements. A degree of goods-received inspection may, therefore, be necessary, if this is the only way that confidence in the supplier's ability to supply to order can be gained.

It may be totally unnecessary to carry out any inspection other than identification and counting, if the supplier is certified either through a third-party registrar or the company's certification program. On the other hand, it may be essential to follow through with 100-percent inspection practices. Only the customer and/or management can decide what is appropriate and acceptable in a particular case.

One of the benefits of appropriate and accurate identification and traceability (clause 4.8) comes into play here. It is acceptable to release material from receipt into production if there is a means to recall it should it subsequently be found to be incorrect. However, this could be an expensive risk to take on many grounds, most of them obvious.

Clause 4.10.3. In-process inspection and testing. During the manufacturing process management must ensure that the product is checked, either by direct measurement or by monitoring of the process. It must not allow the product to proceed unless the required inspections have been carried out and the product approved.

During manufacturing there are stages at which it is prudent to check progress, whether by an initial sample run (ISR) or by inspection, before very costly processing is done. These stages need to be defined on the manufacturing documents in the control system. Material must be prevented from proceeding to these operations unless shown to be acceptable. In the automotive industry, one of the most appropriate tools to use for such an identification is the control plan.

Clause 4.10.4. Final inspection and testing. The final inspection is performed prior to release for delivery. A company must ensure that all necessary tests have been done and that they are documented as such. Nonconforming product, which can occur at each stage of inspection, must be identified as such.

Clause 4.10.5. Inspection and test records. The requirement in clause 4.10.5 is to provide formal proof of the inspection and tests against the criteria that formed the product specification.

Clause 4.11. Control of inspection, measuring, and test equipment. One of the most detailed clauses in the standard is clause 4.11. It reconfirms the need of establishing and maintaining documentation for calibration, inspection, measuring, and testing equipment (4.11.1). Essentially, the clause asks for appropriate and applicable information about the equipment used for measuring acceptability of the product. The second section of the clause (4.11.2) describes nine specific areas in which the supplier should be sure to have formal documentation to demonstrate valid results.

If inspection or test of a product is carried out to determine its acceptability to specified requirements, then the inspection or testing equipment must be capable of giving a valid measurement. The following considerations are necessary.

1. *Register of equipment.* All equipment used to measure and test needs to be listed. Not all equipment needs to be calibrated, so the list must describe which items must be calibrated.

2. *Plan.* Plainly, a rolling plan is necessary so that all equipment does not require recalibrating at the same time. Not all equipment will need the same frequency. Any portable equipment in constant use is likely to need more frequent calibration than pieces used in a controlled environment.

3. *Accuracy tolerances.* A piece of equipment used to make a measurement is chosen based on the product tolerance. The measuring equipment itself has errors. In cases where these errors could give an invalid product measurement, the measuring equipment is not capable. These tolerances and errors need to be determined.

4. *Instructions and records.* Calibration has formal needs for procedures and records of the checks. Actual values attained must be documented. The designations *OK* or a check mark are not acceptable as a record.

5. *Traceability to national standards.* The standards used to check measuring equipment must be related to a national standard. In cases where this is not possible, a written agreement with the customer should define acceptable procedures.

6. *Indication of calibration status.* It must be possible to determine the calibration status of each piece of equipment. This can be accomplished by affixing labels or using color codes, although this is not always possible.

The standard requires that, within the manual or procedures, a company has a method for deciding what it will do if a piece of equipment is found to be out of calibration (which means it has probably passed unacceptable product).

Clause 4.12. Inspection and test status. One of the most self-explanatory clauses of the standard is 4.12. Where a product is likely to have a different status (that is, not inspected, inspected and passed, inspected and rejected, held, and so on), it must be clear. Tags, labels, or accompanying documentation can provide status identification. Particular locations may also facilitate the identification process, as can certain containers specified for unusable items or scrap.

The context of this requirement is related to products, but the principle should be inherent throughout the system. The requirement is to make it clear that an item is unchecked, checked and accepted, or checked and rejected, so that only properly approved items will be used.

Clause 4.13. Control of nonconforming product

Clause 4.13.1. General. As a result of inspection *at any stage* a product may be deemed as nonconforming. Nonconforming product must be prevented from being used until a decision has been made about it. It must be marked and documented. Whenever anything occurs that does not conform with specified requirements, people need to be made aware of it.

Clause 4.13.2. Review and disposition of nonconforming product. When a nonconformance is found, someone must decide how to proceed. Who can make this decision and what he or she may decide must be defined in writing in the quality manual and/or procedures.

Several possibilities exist for the disposition of nonconforming product. The authorized company representative or the customer (if the nonconformance affects customer requirements) might determine that the nonconforming product can be used as is (a waiver is necessary in either of these cases). In some cases, the product can be reworked in order to bring it into conformance with specifications. The nonconforming product might be downgraded for use in certain limited applications. In this case, the specific acceptable applications must be identified and instructions for control must be produced. If none of these situations exists, the product must be scrapped.

Clause 4.14. Corrective action. Clause 4.14 is defined in three subclauses. The first (4.14.1), which is the general one, focuses on implementing a corrective and preventive action. The second (4.14.2) prescribes the essential elements of the corrective action, and the third (4.14.3) prescribes the essential elements of the prevention action. The important issue of this clause is that a potential non-conformance must be corrected for both the short and long terms. If a company is wondering whether to implement certain systems but ignore others, then this requirement should be considered as the one to have above all others.

Any product nonconformance, customer return, complaint, system deficiency, and so on is a failure of the company's management system. Any company wishing to correct any of the problems identified needs to record them, determine the root cause(s) (rather than the symptoms), identify alternative solutions, select the appropriate solution, and monitor the solution for improvement and consistency.

Good records of product and process characteristics help to identify potential problem areas. Therefore, all nonconformances, from whatever source, need to be collated and analyzed.

It is of paramount importance to recognize that the standard does not prescribe what kind of corrective action the company will define. Rather, the standard defines as a requirement the need for and demonstration of a system that is appropriate, applicable, and useful in the definition and solution of a problem.

Clause 4.15. Handling, storage, packaging, preservation, and delivery. At all stages throughout a company, the product is moved, stored, packed, preserved, and then delivered. Each of these actions has its own dangers. The requirement is to determine what the dangers are at each of the stages and then to establish and maintain appropriate documentation within the company's system.

- *Handling.* Different products require different handling. For instance, cleanliness is crucial in the food industry, but impossible in iron founding; and delicate electronic items require electrostatic precautions. Whatever the requirements, they must be formally defined in general or specific procedures and made to work.

- *Storage.* Storage must maintain items in the condition in which they entered the storage area. Security may be important in some companies, with only certain people authorized to enter stores. Of course, storage applies to any parts or items held between stages of processing, so total security may be impossible. Control over passage in and out of storage is essential. The principles of first in, first out stock checking; kanban; and just-in-time inventory are examples of good storage practices. Separation of visually similar items with specified nonconformances are a practical necessity.

- *Packaging.* Packaging must protect the product until it reaches the customer. If used to sell and present the product, it needs to last longer. Usually there are standard packaging requirements for any product unless a customer specifies differently.

- *Preservation.* Preservation methods must be established and maintained for the product as long as it is under the supplier's control.

- *Delivery.* While the extent of responsibility regarding delivery may vary from contract to contract, the company needs to ensure that the delivery method is consistent with protection needed. For example, certain items can be carried in the open air, others must be protected from damp, dirt, rust, shock, and so on.

Clause 4.16. Quality records. In most cases, quality records are the ordinary documents and records produced in each department of the company.

Clause 4.17. Internal quality audits. In order to provide verification evidence of the systems operation, audits of all the activities outlined in the quality manual need to be carried out. A chart displaying the departments down one side and the months of the year across the top is a typical way to portray the data. The audits are carried out against checklists, which are samples taken from the requirements of instructions, procedures, the quality manual, or a standard. The actual operation and effectiveness of those requirements are then checked in practice.

Any areas that are not being operated as the procedures state are recorded as being deficient. Corrective action will either change the way a process is working or the written procedure itself to reflect the current practice. Although the quality assurance department is generally in charge of the audit, it is not essential that audits are done by quality assurance.

What is important is that, because the audit is a verification activity, independence of the auditor from the activity being audited is essential. This independence may be ensured by having a representative of another department perform the audit. It is good practice to allow many people to carry out internal auditing as it increases people's knowledge about the company as a whole and removes the interdepartmental barriers that are so often erected in companies.

The internal audit can be a powerful management tool and is undertaken in much the same way as an audit by a second or third party. Audits look at the whole system and verify whether there is a system, whether it is put into practice, and whether it is effective. The audits must react to the needs of the system and include follow-up of any area found to be deficient in any way. Any deficiencies found must be reported to management responsible for that area.

Clause 4.18. Training. The intent of clause 4.18, in general, is to establish the requirements for training, certifying, and recertifying employees involved in performing critical and specialized functions at a given organization. Specifically, this paragraph focuses on the following questions.

- Does the training program cover quality awareness for the entire organization?

  —How are the training needs identified?

  —Is the top management included in this training?

  —Are the objectives of the training appropriate with what is really required?

- Does the training program cover the development of special skills required for various processes, including the qualifications or certification of the personnel, where applicable?

  —How are the qualifications determined (through education, training, experience, or a combination of these)?

  —How is management training and development identified? How is it carried out?

- How does the training program cover the requirements for requalification, certification, or recertification?

  —Is formal education necessary?

  —Is a vocational school appropriate?

  —Is the apprenticeship program certified?

  —Are the requirements for qualification, requalification, certification, and recertification appropriate for the skills of the organization?

- How are the instructors/trainers selected?

  —How do they get qualified?

  —Is there a certification program?

- What records are kept of the results of the training?

  —Are training procedures available and controlled? Why or why not?

—Are the results of training monitored and documented to show verifiable achievement?

—Are all training records/procedures legible, identifiable, and retrievable?

• Are retention times established and recorded?

—How was the retention time established? Is it appropriate? Why or why not?

• Are the procedures, documents, and records available to the customer (if they are contractual agreements)?

• Is there a budget allocation for training?

—Is technical training provided (skills updated)?

—Is orientation part of the general training?

—What constitutes normal training?

Although 4.18 is very specific and focuses on the issues of training of a special nature, the intent and scope of the paragraph are more than the explicit identification. The requirement covers all employees performing routine, critical, and specialized functions related to deliverable items. This includes both management and nonmanagement personnel. In addition to this general impact, the clause may also include requirements specified by the customer's contract.

The concerns and implications of 4.18 may be frightening to some companies. In reality, though, they are nothing more than a substantiation of the quality system that the company itself has defined in its own quality manual. The ingredients identified in the quality manual ought to be

• Identification of training needs

• Training program

• Records

Clause 4.19. Servicing. Clause 4.19 is a unique clause in the standard because it is conditional upon whether a contract requires servicing. If a contract requires servicing, then the means must exist to ensure that the servicing is done as required by the contract.

Service personnel need to be kept advised of new products and competitors' information. Service staff are at the sharp end, often dealing with frustrated users of the product. Their reports are of real-life situations and, in most cases, these reports are extremely valuable.

Clause 4.20. Statistical techniques. The statistical techniques requirement is perhaps the most misunderstood clause of the standard. It is assumed by most to mean that specific statistical charting and traditional statistical process control must be performed. Nothing could be further from the truth. What it does state is that an identification of need is to be established (4.20.1) and then appropriate procedures should be maintained (4.20.2) to implement and control the application of 4.20.1.

This clause encourages management to consider ways of determining process capability and to review current methods of inspection. Furthermore, it encourages the use of statistical methods, that is, control charts, sampling techniques, descriptive statistics, and anything that is applicable, appropriate, and useful for the organization and, more specifically, for the process. In addition, this clause is written as encouragement to companies to utilize any statistical techniques that will identify, measure, control, and monitor the variation of the process.

Any pure quality assurance program can be viewed as the removal of undesirable variables from the process, whatever that process is. In today's environment this principle is essential, but the traditional sampling tables are not adequate to control products down to parts per million or parts per billion levels. As a consequence, other approaches are necessary.

Comparison of the Certifiable Standards

While the ISO 9001, 9002, and 9003 standards provide specific requirements for certification in different situations, all of them have common clauses. Specifically, ISO 9001 has 20 clauses, ISO 9002 has 19, and ISO 9003 has 16 clauses. The 16 clauses found

Table 3.1. Hierarchy and comparison of the ISO 9000 series standards.

Standard	Clause	Description
ISO 9001 (20 elements)	4.4	Design control
	4.19	Servicing
ISO 9002 (19 elements)	4.9	Process control
	4.6	Purchasing
	4.20	Statistical techniques
	4.18	Training
	4.17	Quality audits
	4.16	Control of quality records
	4.15	Handling, storage, packaging, preservation, and delivery
	4.14	Corrective and preventive action
	4.13	Control of nonconforming product
	4.12	Inspection and test status
	4.11	Control of inspection, measuring, and test equipment
ISO 9003 (16 elements)	4.10	Inspection and testing
	4.8	Product identification and traceability
	4.7	Control of customer-supplied product
	4.5	Document and data control
	4.3	Contract review
	4.2	Quality system
	4.1	Management responsibility

in ISO 9003 are found in all the standards and constitute the basis for the structure in the quality system. ISO 9002 includes three more than ISO 9003, which are also included in ISO 9001. ISO 9001 includes one more clause than ISO 9002. ISO 9001 is the most complete and stringent standard out of the three ISO 9000 series certifiable standards. Each clause and its description is found in Table 3.1 on the preceding page.

All three standards begin the actual certifiable requirements at clause (section) 4.0. The first three sections deal with introduction, scope, and references and definitions.

ISO 9001 requires that a company plans for quality, follows through on this plan, and documents the system. The standard also requires the company to audit and review what it has done against the objectives and take action on any differences. In reviewing ISO 9001, one can appreciate the fact that the requirements are extensive, but also extremely flexible. They allow a company much leeway, provided that the documentation is defined and exists for whatever the company has deemed necessary.

Reference

Chrysler Corporation, Ford Motor Company, and General Motors Corporation. 1994. *Quality systems assessment.* Southfield, Mich.: Chrysler Corporation, Ford Motor Company, and General Motors Corporation.

QS-9000: The Revised Automotive Requirements

Chapter 4 supplements Chapter 3. It addresses the additional requirements that are necessary for a proper certification in the automotive industry. It explains each of the elements separately and gives some guidelines for conformance. A few of the clauses are self-explanatory and, as such, they do not need any editorial comment(s). For official interpretations, readers are encouraged to obtain the most recent copy of the IASG-sanctioned interpretations.

Overview

The U.S. automotive industry has been trying to harmonize standards and processes for about 10 years. The first major effort was to agree to using the same shipping labels so that suppliers would not have to buy three different systems to get their products into the auto manufacturer's plants. Today, a number of quality-related documents produced by Chrysler, Ford, and GM have also been harmonized, including: *Measurement Systems Analysis: Reference Manual* (1995b), *Statistical Process Control: Reference Manual* (1995f), *Production Part Approval Process* (1995d), *Potential Failure Mode and Effects Analysis: Reference Manual* (1995c), and *Advanced Product Quality Planning and Control Plan: Reference Manual* (1995a).

Effective August 1994, a quality systems document called *Quality System Requirements: QS-9000,* known simply as QS-9000 (Chrysler, Ford, and GM 1994c), became available and required for all suppliers to the U.S. automotive manufacturers as well as some heavy truck manufacturers. However, European and Asian automotive transplants have yet to agree on the use of QS-9000 or any of the other manuals now available through the Task Force and distributed by Chrysler, Ford, and GM. The introduction of these quality system requirements created a great demand, and at the same time, some confusion was generated in certain elements due to inappropriate clarification. As a result of this confusion, the Task Force released the second edition to QS-9000 effective February 1995 (Chrysler, Ford, and GM 1995e). As of this writing, the group that is responsible for distributing these harmonized manuals including the QS-9000 in the United States is the AIAG.

This chapter focuses on the QS-9000 second edition. It uses ISO 9001, Section 4 as the foundation and adds interpretations and supplemental quality system requirements to develop a harmonized format for the Big Three. The effort replaces the separate documents used by each of the Big Three firms up to this point. The documents that have been replaced include Chrysler's *Supplier Quality Assurance Manual,* Ford's *Q-101 Quality System Standard,* and General Motor's North American Operations (NAO) *Targets for Excellence.*

As in the first edition, the ISO 9001 text is reproduced verbatim in italic type while the additional requirements are printed in normal block type. Both the ISO and some of the accreditation bodies, such as RAB and RvA, have agreed to allow the usage of QS-9000 in the automotive industry. (There are rumors that QS-9000 may also be used in other industries as well. Furthermore, the trend seems to be that specific industries such as travel, education, textile, and software are in the process of developing their own industry standards.)

Since QS-9000 was introduced, much discussion has been devoted to the issue of what it is and what it can do. To find the answer, look at the introduction to the requirements. It states on page 1 that "the goal for QS-9000 is the development of fundamental quality systems that provide for continuous improvement, emphasizing defect prevention and the reduction of variation and waste in the supply chain" (Chrysler, Ford, and GM 1995e). In essence then, QS-9000 is a quality system that provides the means by which this goal of continual improvement can be met.

Of special interest is the situation of the suppliers of equipment suppliers, warehouses, service suppliers, and other nonproduction suppliers to the automotive industry. These suppliers should take note that plans are being developed to include them at a future date in some form of harmonized quality systems effort. In fact, a supplement has already been published for the semiconductor industry for both the QS-9000 document and the quality system assessment. (The Task Force, as of this writing, is working on a supplement for tooling and equipment suppliers.) This does not mean that all suppliers should immediately acquire an ISO 9000 registration (unless specified by your customer), because any supplier now registered to ISO 9001 or ISO 9002 is not qualified under QS-9000.

In fact, *any* supplier currently registered to ISO 9001, ISO 9002, or ISO 9003 is not qualified under QS-9000. This is because *the requirements of ISO 9000 and QS-9000 are not the same.* The QS-9000 requirements are much more specific and prescriptive than the ISO 9000 series certifiable standards, with more than 100 additional requirements. For example, in the 1987 version of ISO 9001, you could count 113 individual "shall" statements that were requirements and became auditable by a registrar. The new 1994 revision includes 134 "shall" statements.

In QS-9000 Section I there are 231 "shall" statements with an additional 13 "shall" statements in Section II, which are specific automotive requirements, auditable by third-party registrars. Thus, if you are registered to ISO 9001, the registrar only audited 130 items. On the other hand, if your registrar is qualified to conduct QS-9000 registration audits, the required "shall" plus the additional other requirements (such as "must," "is required," and "will") number more than 300 auditable items. This may seem as a little excessive to some organizations, but both ISO and the Task Force view the additional requirements as a clarification to the original ISO 9001 elements.

One additional note before we look at the specifics of QS-9000. In the process of counting the "shall" words in the document, a writing evaluation software package was used to ensure that an exact count was achieved. The readability index was also calculated (using the Fog Index method) on the QS-9000 document, which includes ISO 9001, Section 4. The results of this software study indicate that readers need a seventeenth-grade level of education (five years of college work), which implies that the writing is complex and may be difficult to read and understand. Therefore, it is imperative that any company planning to use either ISO 9001 or QS-9000 should take extra precautions to clearly understand the requirements.

The QS-9000 document is written in three parts or sections. Section I: ISO 9000-Based Requirements include the ISO information verbatim with the addition of automotive information included in block type. All 20 elements found in ISO 9001 are found in this section. Section II: Chrysler, Ford, and GM Requirements consists of three basic sections covering the production part approval process, continuous improvement, and manufacturing capabilities. These items are not found in the ISO 9000 series but are required to do business in the U.S. automotive industry. Section III: Customer-Specific Requirements is in four parts, one for each of the Big Three automotive companies and one for truck manufacturers. There are some new changes here. (All the detailed changes were listed in

Chapter 1.) The section for Chrysler is third-party auditable now; however, suppliers have to be registered by July 31, 1997. As of this writing, Ford does not require a third-party registration, but does require compliance to QS-9000. The section for General Motors is third-party auditable now; however, suppliers have to be registered by December 31, 1997. The truck manufacturers' requirements are still individualized; however, suppliers should contact the individual truck manufacturer's purchasing department for the most current information.

The requirements presented in Section III are specific items each company wants from its suppliers and the concepts are, in fact, covered by most of the requirements found in Sections I and II. Specific procedures, terms, methods, and activities are mentioned in Section III to be used by suppliers to that specific company. Eight appendixes are found in the back of the QS-9000 document covering The Quality System Assessment Process, Code of Practice, Specific Characteristics and Symbols, Local Equivalents for ISO 9001 and 9002 Specifications, Acronyms and Their Meanings, Change Summary, QS-9000 Accreditation Body Implementation Requirements, Survey Audit Days Table, and a Glossary.

Other items in the introduction include the applicability, implementation, and quality system documentation progression. QS-9000 is applicable to *all* internal and external suppliers of production and service parts and heat treating, painting, plating or other finishing services supplied to the U.S. automotive industry. Thus, all tier one suppliers must meet these requirements. In addition, all tier one suppliers are required to develop their suppliers, the tier two supplier base, using QS-9000. With the original distribution of the QS-9000 document, as well as the revised one in February 1995, all specific quality system standards used by the individual automotive original equipment manufacturers (OEMs) have been superseded.

The designation of tier one versus tier two in the U.S. automotive supplier base refers to whether a supplier ships products directly to one of the Big Three or to other suppliers. Tier one suppliers are those that ship directly to the automotive assembly plants. Tier two suppliers are those companies that supply to the tier one suppliers. Tier three suppliers would be those shipping to tier two, and so on back into the supply chain as far as needed to complete the material supply. There are cases in which some suppliers can be both tier one and tier two depending on their customer base.

As of this writing, the implementation specifics have not been completely worked out. Basically, GM and Chrysler have announced that they are out of the auditing business. Ford, on the other hand, will rely on either second- or third-party audits. It is imperative for suppliers to understand that they must use registrars carefully. They should select an auditor specifically approved by a national registration body for QS-9000 and meeting and/or exceeding the requirements stated in the Code of Practice as outlined in Appendix B of the QS-9000 document. Furthermore, the registrars must meet the QS-9000 accreditation body implementation requirements as delineated in Appendix G. In all cases, registration through a qualified third party will be accepted and it will be up to the supplier to share such registration with each of its customers.

As of this writing, the QS-000 approved accreditation bodies are as follows:

Accreditation body	Country
RAB	United States
RvA	Netherlands
UKAS	United Kingdom
JAS-ANZ	Australia/New Zealand
SWEDAC	Sweden
TGA	Germany

SAS	Switzerland
SINCERT	Italy
FINAS	Finland
SCC	Canada
ENAC	Spain

In addition, Chrysler, Ford, and GM have announced that certificates issued by registrars that are accredited by one or more of the following QS-9000 qualified registrars will be recognized.

Registrar	Office qualified	Accrediting body
ABS	Texas	RvA, RAB
BSI	United Kingdom	RvA
DNV	Texas	RAB
Entela	Michigan	RvA, RAB
KPMG	New Jersey	RvA, RAB
LRQA	New Jersey	RAB
LRQA	United Kingdom	RvA
NSF	Michigan	RvA
OMNEX	Michigan	RAB
QMI	Canada	RvA
Smithers	Ohio	RvA
SRI	Pennsylvania	RvA, RAB
TUV Rheinland	Connecticut	RvA
UL	New York	RvA, RAB

Note: Readers are strongly advised to contact ASQC to get the IASG-sanctioned interpretations for the most up-to-date lists of accreditation bodies and registrars.

The quality system documentation procedures identify how to document a supplier's process. The international standards and customer requirements are called out as the starting point. The QS-9000 document and the PPAP manual are currently the specific contractual requirements published by U.S. OEMs. The other reference manuals (APQP, FMEA, MSA, and Fundamental SPC) are identified as guides to the supplier's process. However, due to the fact that the APQP manual is directly called for in Element 4.2.3 and indirectly in several elements, this makes the APQP manual—by default—a third contractual document. Individual suppliers will have a four-level approach to documenting their quality systems: a quality manual, procedures, job instructions, and other documentation (see Figure 4.1).

Quality manuals define the approach and responsibility of the supplier's quality system. For those suppliers that need additional information about the manual, the ISO 10013 guideline is available (ANSI/ISO/ASQC 1995). It defines the requirements on how to set up a quality manual. Procedures define the who, what, and when within the quality system and must be kept up-to-date at the point of use throughout the system. Job instructions answer how individuals do their work. These are required for all employees responsible for operating processes. Other documentation will be required as deemed necessary to run the operation system, including the results of how the system is operating. Other documentation is often embedded in either procedures and/or job instructions. Typically other documentation may be in the form of forms, tags, stamps, and so on. A visual representation of this can be seen in Figure 4.1.

Note: Ford requires its suppliers to run their business operating system using what Ford refers to as a "quality operating system (QOS)." QOS is defined as "a systematic, disciplined approach that uses standardized tools and practices to manage the business and achieve ever-increasing levels of customer satisfaction through continual process improvement." Many suppliers to Ford are being

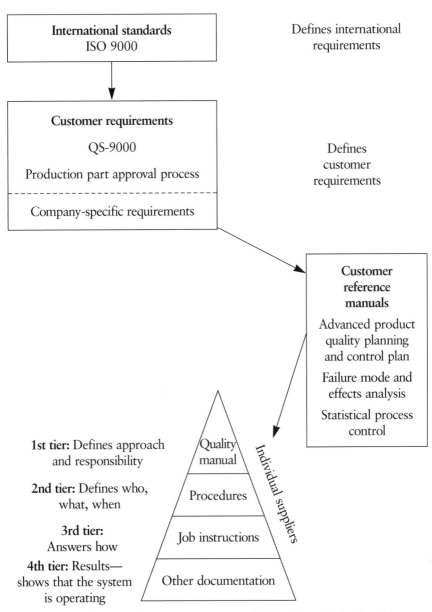

Source: Modified from *Quality System Requirements: QS-9000.* Chrysler, Ford, and GM. Used with permission.

Figure 4.1. Quality system documentation progression.

audited separately to the Ford *QOS Assessment & Rating Procedure* (1993a), which is referred to but not included in the QS-9000 requirements.

Section I: ISO 9000-Based Requirements

In Chapter 3, I discussed the elements of ISO 9001 in detail. In this section, I will address only the additional requirements of each element for the automotive industry as identified in the QS-9000 system. Each element will be identified separately to help readers who are using this as a reference for future questions about QS-9000.

Element 4.1. Management Responsibility

The additional requirements of this element are found in Element 4.1.2.3, Management Representative, dealing with the organizational interface.

Two areas of requirements are added. One is that, during the concept development, prototype, and production phase of a new part, a system of management is to be in place to ensure the quality of the part. And second, a multidisciplinary approach to decision making is to be used, with information and data communicated to the customer in customer-prescribed formats. Examples of functions are given in the included note.

Management Review (4.1.3). This element mandates the necessity for a management review of the entire quality system.

Business Plan (4.1.4). The content of this requirement is not auditable by a third-party registrar but may be requested by the customer. This element requires that a formal, documented, comprehensive business plan be developed by the supplier. It is imperative for suppliers to understand that the auditors must verify that the supplier is conducting strategic business planning with appropriate initiatives. Proof, such as a dated table of contents and a review of nonsensitive sections (IASG 1995, 28), is required. Examples of items to be included are given and a number of recommendations are listed for consideration. The recommendations are not an exhaustive list but rather examples of possibilities.

The recommendations are considered very standard items for any well-run organization, and it has been reported that at least one major lending institution in southeastern Michigan has approached Ford Motor Company asking to benchmark how Ford reviews suppliers. The financial institution indicated that, of those companies that had loans with the institution and listed Ford as a customer, these companies had some of the soundest business practices and the lowest default rates within the financial system.

Analysis and Use of Company-Level Data (4.1.5). Suppliers to U.S. OEMs are required to maintain records and show the data in trend format of how the business is operating in the areas of quality, operational performances, and current quality levels for key product and service features. While QS-9000 does not refer to any specific approach for analysis and use of data, I think that an excellent example is the QOS used by Ford Motor Company (Ford 1994b). QOS is based on the principle of collecting and evaluating existing data into a system of key processes and result measurables that are correlated and can be quickly reviewed and acted on through an appropriate corrective action.

Customer Satisfaction (4.1.6). Suppliers are required to have documented processes for determining customer satisfaction with consideration to objectivity and validity of such data. Also, data and records are required to be shown in trend format to illustrate continual improvement efforts in the supplier quality system. Some of the most typical tools (techniques, methods) used for identifying customer satisfaction are

- Quality function deployment
- Benchmarking
- Focus groups
- Audits
- Surveys

Element 4.2. Quality System

The additional requirements of this element are found in clause 4.2.3 dealing with quality planning. A number of specific items that suppliers are required to use are referenced in this element. They are as follows:

Quality Planning—Direction is given to suppliers advising them that they must use the *Advanced Product Quality Planning and Control Plan: Reference Manual* (Chrysler, Ford, and GM 1995a). This manual is available through AIAG and, with this requirement, the manual is virtually raised to customer requirement status on a par with the *Production Part Approval Process* manual.

APQP is a structured procedure for defining, establishing, and specifying goals for product quality levels and methods for realization. It is also a systematic approach used to identify improvement opportunities in the product design, process design, preproduction, and production stages of the product cycle.

On the other hand, the PPAP document covers generic requirements for production part approval for all production and service commodities, including bulk materials. The requirements identified within the PPAP manual apply equally when these commodities are produced internally by the automotive manufacturers or externally by outside suppliers.

Special Characteristics—OEMs have specific guidelines about how to develop FMEAs and control plans and what is to be included. Reference on this procedure is given in Section III and Appendix C of QS-9000 and the FMEA and APQP manuals. Remember, cross-functional teams are required to develop the plans, and both are to be living documents in the supplier's QOS.

Special characteristics are a result of the quality planning activities that define special product and/or process characteristics resulting from understanding the "voice of the customer."

Use of Cross-Functional Teams—The supplier should establish and implement teams during the APQP process for all new parts. The foundation for the cross-functionality is based on the principle of synergy. While the standards call for the existence of teams, the direction of how to form them is left to the individual company.

Feasibility Reviews—Whether or not a manufacturing company can produce the proposed product(s) is to be determined in the very early stages of the planning process for new parts. Suppliers are required to ensure that planning is done early in the process to prevent surprises after hard tooling is cut and ready for production. Part of the feasibility review is to identify the suitability of a particular design. Typical approaches to feasibility may be capability studies and/or design review.

Process Failure Mode and Effects Analysis (Process FMEA)—A process FMEA is a disciplined review and analysis of a new/revised process and is conducted to anticipate, resolve, or monitor potential process problems. At all times remember that the FMEA is a living document and needs to be reviewed and updated as new failures are discovered.

In this subclause, two requirements are emphasized. First, look at all special characteristics of the new part and ensure that improvements to the process are instituted before production even starts. The OEMs are looking for continual improvement in all stages of the production process, especially in trying to push improvements earlier and earlier in the development process of a new part. For more information on FMEA see Stamatis (1995) and Chrysler, Ford, and GM (1995c).

The second requirement is the *control plan,* a description of the dimensional measurements and material and functional tests that will occur after prototype and before full production. Its primary function is to aid the manufacturing process for a quality product based on customer requirements. It does this by providing a structured approach for the design, selection, and implementation of value-added control methods for the total system (Chrysler, Ford, and GM 1995a, 33).

Until now, there have been few reference documents explaining how to use control plans. Many people have never even seen a control plan. With the publication of the APQP manual, and other sources such as SAE (1994) and Stamatis (1995), the OEMs have a reference manual and texts that explain what control plans are and how to use them. In this element of QS-9000, suppliers are required to develop control plans for all new parts. Also, due to the fact that these documents are to be living documents—changed anytime something changes in the part or the system that builds or manufactures the part—three distinct control plans are identified: prototype, prelaunch, and production control plans. Records of each level for each new part are required. Again, cross-functional teams are required to develop these documents and, in some cases, these teams will have direct involvement with subcontractors and/or customers.

Control plans are living documents that are required to be updated regularly and at least when the product is changed, the processes are changed, the processes become statistically unstable, and/or when the processes become noncapable. For additional information, see the SPC manual (Ford, Chrysler, and GM 1995f) for direction on stability and capability.

Element 4.3. Contract Review

No new requirements have been added to this element, although this element itself is new to the U.S. automotive industry. Suppliers should be aware that quality is everyone's job. It does not belong to or take place just on the manufacturing floor or in the quality department. This may be a new concept for many organizations today.

The purpose of contract review is to ensure that the company and supplier have the same understanding of the contractual requirements, that the resources of the supplier are adequate to complete the project satisfactorily, and that the review activities are appropriately recorded and kept.

Element 4.4. Design Control

The OEMs have designated this section for only those suppliers with design responsibility. Suppliers that are qualified for ISO 9002 will be required to become registered to QS-9000 with this element deleted. However, for the suppliers who deal with design, some additional requirements are included. How does a supplier determine whether or not it has a design responsibility? The answer is given by IASG (1995, 9).

> If the supplier has the authority to establish a new product specification or change an existing product specification for any product a supplier ships to an OEM customer, then it is design responsible. This requirement for customer approval of changes does not affect this. If this is still unclear, the reader is encouraged to contact customer engineering for further clarification.

In design control the focus is to have a thorough understanding of the requirements and thereby reduce the number of faults (defects, problems, errors) by detecting them at the drawing board. To maximize the development of the design control procedure, a supplier may use a flowchart, beginning with the customer's requirements and finishing with the drawings and/or product depending on the requirements. As part of the flowchart, the supplier should note important milestones of the design process.

Design and Development Planning (4.4.2). Under this clause a strong recommendation (as appropriate) is made to some of the areas that should be covered by the design and development activity. It is common for design companies to prepare a generic checklist to monitor the progress of the design work. That checklist may cover some of the following items.

- An outline of the customer's requirements
- The make-up of the design team and its responsibilities
- The external personnel involved and their input
- Statutory requirements (environmental, liability, and so on)
- A schedule of design review(s)
- Approving authorities (both internal and external)
- The deadline for the project

These are just some examples of items to include on a checklist.

Design Input—Supplemental (4.4.4). Suppliers are required to have appropriate resources and facilities to utilize CAD/CAE, and two-way interfacing should be available with the customer's systems. Typical design inputs are

- Management support
- Design goal(s)
- Reliability and quality goals
- Preliminary block diagram
- Preliminary list of special characteristics
- Product (design) assurance plan

Design Output—Supplemental (4.4.5). This clause is self-explanatory however, it must be emphasized that the supplier's design output must be documented with specific design tools that optimize the design. This element also provides examples of such tools.

Design Verification—Supplemental (4.4.7). The design process, although it appears to be linear, is usually a series of loops comprising proposal, review, improvement, and design. Reviews are critical to the design process because they provide formal occasions for checks and idea generation. They also provide the platform for a wider scope of design input and verification.

Generally speaking, the verification review should examine the following:

- Understanding and meeting the customer's requirements
- The effectiveness of the design (logical testing sequence, reliability)
- The choice of performance of the material specified
- The cost-effectiveness of the design
- Alternate solutions

In this element, suppliers must follow five requirements: (1) Use a comprehensive prototype program unless specifically waived by the customer. (2) Use the same subcontractors during the prototype and production. (3) Conclude the performance testing for product life, reliability, and durability studies. (4) Monitor and conduct all performance testing in a timely fashion to allow the result data to be used by the cross-functional team. (5) Whenever subcontractors are used, provide technical leadership in the development of the part.

Design Changes—Supplemental (4.4.9). Design changes in the course of a project in the automotive industry are inevitable due to the complexity and the duration of the project. The key, then, is good management of the changes so that the impact on the quality, time, and cost of the project is minimized. Critical issues to be concerned with in design change(s) are the following:

- Actions to be taken in the event of change(s)
- Person(s) who authorized change
- Person(s) who approved change(s)
- Effective communication of the changes to all concerned parties

Specifically, two requirements are added to this element: All design changes must have written approval by the customer; and for proprietary designs, studies must be conducted with the customer to ensure that all effects of the change can be properly evaluated.

Element 4.5. Document and Data Control

General—Reference Documents (4.5.1). The supplier is required to have all the latest revisions of any document referenced in drawings, other specification references, and other documents deemed necessary by the customer. Larger suppliers with multiple manufacturing locations must have these documents readily available when requested. Examples of these documents are included in this clause (not an exhaustive list). Of interest is the fact that both the QS-9000 document and business plan must be controlled documents.

Document Identification for Special Characteristics. It is required to use the appropriate characteristic classification. However, customers may use unique symbols to identify important characteristics, such as those that affect customer safety, compliance with regulations, function, fit, or appearance. These characteristics are known as "critical," "key," "safety," "significant," and so on. They may, in fact, be designated in many ways because there is no standard for this designation. However, nonstandard customer-designated special characters must be appropriately noted and labeled on all documents at the supplier's location. A list of common and recommended symbols and identifications can be found in QS-9000 Appendix C, Special Characteristics and Symbols of QS-9000. For a more detailed discussion see Stamatis (1995).

Document and Data Approval and Issue—Engineering Specifications (4.5.2). Three specific items are added to the requirements in this element. (1) Procedures shall be established for timely review, distribution, and implementation of all customer standards/specifications and changes. (2) Maintenance records shall be noted in all of the supplier's documentation. (3) Implementation of changes shall be recorded in the appropriate document. An important note was added to the revised QS-9000 requirements to define timely review.

Element 4.6. Purchasing

General—Approved Materials for Ongoing Production (4.6.1). Suppliers are required to use only approved subcontractors where designations have been made by the customer. Also, all materials and processes used to make parts are required to comply with all governmental regulations. Some examples of governmental regulations that must be satisfied are given as part of the text in the clause.

Evaluation of Subcontractors—Subcontractor Development (4.6.2). Suppliers are required to use QS-9000 Sections I and II to evaluate their subcontractors. This may be accomplished by the customer, a customer-approved OEM second party, or an accredited third-party registrar.

Evaluation of Subcontractors—Scheduling (4.6.2). Three requirements are listed in this part of the element. (1) The subcontractor is required to provide 100-percent on-time delivery. (2) The supplier is required to provide appropriate planning to ensure execution of delivery schedules. (3) The supplier is required to monitor delivery performance, including tracking of premium excessive freight. Keeping track of key suppliers and their deliveries is a very important issue; auditors are keenly aware of this.

Purchasing Data—Restricted Substances (4.6.3). All governmental and safety constraints must be met in dealing with any materials or processes used to produce parts for the customer.

Element 4.7. Control of Customer-Supplied Product

No additional requirements have been added to this element. The revised edition clarifies this element even further with an added note.

Element 4.8. Product Identification and Traceability

A note is given to the "where appropriate" comment in the ISO document: Where appropriate refers to situations in which the product identity is not inherently obvious. In such cases, the supplier must provide adequate identification.

Element 4.9. Process Control

This is one of the most demanding QS-9000 elements. The 1995 edition provides a better clarification. The document provides several additional requirements dealing with three additional conditions.

1. *Governmental safety and environmental regulations.* This added condition deals with satisfying all the safety and environmental issues.

2. *Designation of special characteristics.* Self-explanatory item. No additional comments.

A note is given to explain why some characteristics are identified as special for the production of parts for the customer.

3. *Preventative maintenance.* A total preventative maintenance plan must be in effect for key process equipment. Three areas for special considerations are a procedure, a schedule, and a review of equipment manufacturer's recommendations.

To clarify these conditions, the Task Force has added seven subsections to this element. The focus of the subsections is process control using statistical and other methods. The subsections are as follows.

Process Monitoring and Operator Instructions (4.9.1). All employees responsible for operations of processes, shall have documented process monitoring and operator instructions. The operator instructions should contain at least 13 individual requirements, which are all listed.

Preliminary Process Capability Requirements (4.9.2). Capability studies are required on all preliminary processes, with the results meeting customer requirements. If a study does not meet the requirements, a corrective action plan will be required to improve the process so that the next study will meet the requirements. If no requirements have been specified, a P_{pk} target of 1.67 is to be used for preliminary results (less than 30 production days) and for chronically unstable processes.

A P_{pk} (process performance index) is a variable data measure of a process performance that uses the engineering specifications, the standard deviation of all measured samples taken from the process, and the process mean. Attribute data can be used to help identify process improvements.

For the actual definition of preliminary process performance see the glossary of the QS-9000 document (Chrysler, Ford, and GM 1995e, 98).

Ongoing Process Performance Requirements (4.9.3). This subelement does not have auditable requirements but is designated to clarify the monitoring of ongoing process performance. C_{pk} will typically be used for statistically stable processes. The use of control charts, control plans, and continuous improvement is discussed.

Modified Preliminary or Ongoing Capability Requirements (4.9.4). The customer may change the requirements. If that is the case, then control plans should be used to reflect any changes in process and/or capability requirements.

Verification of Job Setups (4.9.5). Two points are required in this subelement. Job setups are to be verified using statistical methods to ensure that parts produced will meet specifications. The other is that documented instructions shall be available for setup personnel.

Process Changes (4.9.6). The supplier must keep a record of all process changes, according to the PPAP manual.

Appearance Items (4.9.7). If the customer has identified character-istics as appearance items, the supplier is required to have at least four characteristics that are listed in this clause.

Element 4.10. Inspection and Testing

General—Acceptance Criteria (4.10.1). Attribute acceptable sam-pling plans usually allow for defect materials and are not acceptable in the OEM community due to a number of litigations over the years. Thus, suppliers are required to use sampling plans that reflect zero defects (Stamatis 1995; Philo 1993).

Accredited Laboratories. Accredited laboratories are to be used any time these services are specified by the customer.

Receiving Inspection and Testing—Incoming Product Quality (4.10.2). Suppliers should monitor the quality of incoming parts from subcontractors. This clause identifies at least five techniques to follow.

Final Inspection and Testing—Layout Inspection and Functional Testing (4.10.4). Suppliers must have results of layout inspection and functional verifications for review if a customer requests them.

Element 4.11. Control of Inspection, Measuring, and Test Equipment

Two additional subelements are added to the ISO 9001 requirements.

Inspection, Measuring and Test Equipment Records (4.11.3). Records on all (this includes employee-owned) gauges, measuring, and test equipment must have at least the following information.

- Revisions following engineering changes
- Gauge conditions and actual readings as received for calibration/verification
- Notification to customer if suspect materials have been shipped

Measurement System Analysis (4.11.4). There are no specific auditable requirements in this subelement. It does suggest that the suppliers use the *Measurement Systems Analysis: Reference Manual* (Chrysler, Ford, and GM 1995b).

Element 4.12. Inspection and Test Status

Product Location. This subelement is a note relating to location of product and its inspection status. If an in-process product has been placed in a designated location because it did not pass inspection, it must also be identified so that it does not mistakenly get returned with products that have passed inspection and contaminate the finished product.

Supplemental Verification. Customers may require special verification of finished product, and any requirements given by the customer must be adhered to by the supplier.

Element 4.13. Control of Nonconforming Product

General—Suspect Product (4.13.1). Self-explanatory. Two additional subelements have also been added to the ISO 9001 requirement.

Control of Reworked Product (4.13.3). Two components are found in this subelement. Appropriate employees will have access to rework instructions. Also, nonconforming products must be quantified and problems analyzed. A prioritized reduction plan must be prepared. Corrective action plans may be required to prevent the recurrence of such nonconforming material. This clause emphasizes the need for documentation of the reworked product. It does not prescribe the method of the rework and/or the process of the corrective action.

Engineering Approved Product Authorization (4.13.4). The customer must give prior written approval before any changes can be made to a product, or the process that produces the product, that are different than the initial approval received through the part sample warrant. More information on this procedure can be found in *Production Part Approval Process* (Chrysler, Ford, and GM 1995d). Note that this procedure also applies to suspect material.

Element 4.14. Corrective and Preventive Action

General—Problem-Solving Methods (4.14.1). The OEMs use disciplined problem-solving techniques and require suppliers to use such practices. This is especially true when product is sent to the customer that does not meet requirements. The specific problem-solving technique is left to the discretion of the individual company.

Corrective Action—Returned Product Test/Analysis (4.14.2). Three auditable requirements are given in this subelement: Any part(s) returned from the customer must be analyzed; records of these studies must be maintained; and corrective action must be taken to prevent recurrence of the noted nonconformity.

Like other elements of the requirements, this one does not prescribe a specific solution. Rather, this element reiterates the spirit of corrective action and continuous improvement. It also allows the company to define its own procedure(s), method(s), documentation, and reporting.

Element 4.15. Handling, Storage, Packaging, Preservation and Delivery

Storage—Inventory (4.15.3). The supplier is expected to use an effective inventory management system to optimize the process and ensure that fresh stock is always available. A specific process is not required, but the supplier must ensure that the areas of inventory turns, stock rotation, and inventory levels are addressed within the system used. Examples of common inventory systems found in the automotive industry are just-in-time (JIT) and kanban.

Packaging (4.15.4). This subelement addresses two additional requirements. They are

1. *Customer packaging standards.* Any unusual packaging requirements and guidelines must be identified.

2. *Labeling.* Self-explanatory.

Delivery—Supplier Delivery Performance Monitoring (4.15.6). With this clause, the supplier is required to establish a goal of 100-percent on-time delivery to the customer. If a supplier cannot meet this goal, the supplier must implement a system to improve delivery and communicate any problems to the customer. See also comments at Element 4.6.2 dealing with scheduling.

A lead time requirement system must be developed to effectively ensure that the product(s) will be ready to ship on time. This includes a method of monitoring and tracking performance against customer requirements regarding delivery schedules.

Finally, the shipment of all material must meet with all requirements or regulations of the customer and any local, state, and/or national government requirements or regulations.

Production Scheduling. The supplier must develop a procedure for ordering raw materials based on the customers' requirements for production. Techniques using JIT manufacturing and allowing for small production runs are highly encouraged.

Shipment Notification System. The automotive industry uses an advance shipment notification (ASN) system to track shipment of goods. The supplier must be fully software capable in using this system. A back-up system must be in place if the computerized system should fail.

Element 4.16. Control of Quality Records

Record Retention. Generally speaking, most records pertaining to a part will be kept for the life of the production of the part plus one year. The only auditable requirements include

- Quality performance records, which are to be kept for one year from the calendar year in which they were created

- Internal quality system audits and management reviews, which must be retained for three years

Suppose, for example, that you worked on a control chart for a particular part. You have several pages that were produced in September 1995. After December 31, 1996 you may dispose of this documentation, unless otherwise specified by the customer.

This element also requires that the supplier must specify a disposal time. In fact, the auditors have been instructed to look for the disposal time and verify whether or not the disposal actually occurs as defined. If a supplier does not specify the disposal time or the actual disposal cannot be verified, auditors have been instructed to identify these situations as a nonconformance.

Superseded Parts. When a part is replaced by a new part, all documents pertaining to the new part must be kept in a new file, so that records from the two do not become mixed.

Element 4.17. Internal Quality Audits

Inclusion of Working Environment. When conducting internal quality system audits, the supplier must include information on employees' working conditions in the audit.

It has been known for a long time that a high correlation exists between the working environment that management provides for employees and the quality system that produces parts for shipment. This is why you will find that some auditors check bathrooms first as they enter a production area. It has been said that

"If management can't even keep the washroom clean and orderly, how can it deliver a quality product to the customer?"

Element 4.18. Training

Training as a Strategic Issue. One requirement is added requiring periodic evaluation of training effectiveness. Suppliers are also encouraged to view training as a strategic issue.

With this addition by the U.S. automotive industry, a complete training package may soon be required using the technology found in the field of instructional system design. This field deals with training interventions and at a minimum involves needs assessment, design, development, implementation, and evaluation of training. This field is commonly referred to as *instructional technology.*

Ford has already developed such a program and Chrysler is currently working with United Automobile Workers (UAW) to develop a similar one. GM, as of this writing, has not developed anything similar to this. The Ford program, called *Ford Instructional Systems Design Process,* is already offered to Ford employees and the supplier base (Cvercko, Antonelli, and Steele 1992).

Element 4.19. Servicing

Feedback on Information from Service. When the supplier has some serviceability requirements for the customer, a system of communication must be in place to notify all of the necessary departments within the supplier's company.

Element 4.20. Statistical Techniques

Selection of Statistical Tools (4.20.2). Supplier personnel are expected to know about statistical tools and how to use them in various applications of the business. Where appropriate, these tools must be mentioned in the control plans.

Knowledge of Basic Statistical Concepts. This item is a recommendation to suppliers but it is expected that everyone in the organization understands how four items (variation, stability versus unstable conditions, capability, and over-adjustment) affect their working environment.

Even through the knowledge of basic statistical concepts does not contain an auditable requirement at this point, an experienced auditor can and will check to see if the supplier's employees are applying sound techniques.

Using Control Charts as Part of the SPC Program. For the last 14 years in the automotive world, it has been the default modus operandi to expect some kind of statistical process control (charting, C_{pk}, and so on). In the ISO 9000 and QS-9000 world, the application of SPC may or may not be necessary. What is necessary is that the process be controlled and the use of some kind of advanced quality planning must be in place. It is implied that SPC be used as part of Element 4.20 but it is not mandated in any way, shape, or form. On the other hand, the use of SPC in a given organization may be a contractual agreement between the company and the supplier or customer. To emphasize this very point, the QS-9000 manual on page 49 in the last paragraph makes the following reference: "Consult the *Fundamental Statistical Process Control: Reference Manual.*" The implication here is that it may very well be necessary for your company to use SPC, but then again it may not. If the organization fulfills the requirements defined by the customer, and all the requirements of the SPC reference manual have been followed, then SPC may indeed be an overkill.

New to SPC? Using SPC is a reliable means for gathering accurate and detailed information that can aid in making decisions affecting quality, productivity, customer service, and cost reduction. SPC often has been acknowledged as a set of tools that is helping all kinds of organizations become more effective and therefore more competitive by raising quality standards and quality awareness in an organization.

When implementing an SPC program, the initial step is to begin identifying the various possible causes of the nonconforming items in the work environment. This is typically completed during a brainstorming session of the people involved. This type of session should ideally involve five to nine people who know and understand the task. Because they know and understand the task they can *best* contribute potential solutions to problems. The reason for the brainstorming is to generate as many possible alternatives to the task. Once the brainstorming is complete, the information is organized into logical categories. Sometimes this can be done during the brainstorming activity—generally known as the 5M's and E (machine, method, material, manpower, measurement, and environment). Categories are then organized into a diagram known as a fishbone diagram, Ishikawa diagram, or cause-and-effect diagram.

The next step is to define the data that the team will need to resolve the nonconformity. Then the team needs to begin collecting data, keeping two specific points in mind. First, all processes generate data. Second, all data are of two types: (1) Measurable or variable data, which are data that can be measured. (2) Attribute or counted data, which are data that can be counted. The use of specific statistical tools will be determined by the kinds of data one has.

The next step in implementing the SPC program is to establish which problem has *the* priority based on frequency, dissatisfaction, cost, or any other attribute that your organization and/or management has set for a priority. The process for prioritization is called *Pareto analysis.*

The analysis of the data follows. Depending on the data available, a control chart is developed. Usual charts are the X-bar and R, cusum, standard deviation and R, moving range, and c, p, u, and *np* charts. The essence of all the charts is to identify changes in the process. The changes can be either good or bad. The determination of the good or bad change can be done if, and only if, you know the characteristic you are monitoring and understand the concept of variation.

To make a good decision, the concept of variation must be understood. Variation exists in all processes and in everything we do. Nobody, or no one, or anything is perfect or exactly alike. Our task, then, is to differentiate the variation we can live with and the variation we cannot live with. The control chart does precisely that. We call the variation we can live with "normal," "inherent," or "common" and it is usually between the limits of the control charts. We call the variation we cannot live with "assignable cause" or "special," and it is usually outside the limits of the control charts. When variation is noted to be outside the control limits—and, under some special conditions, inside the control limits—we call the process "out of control" or "unstable." When variation is within the control limits without any special abnormalities, we call the process "in control" and "stable." To implement SPC in a given organization, the following minimum requirements are necessary.

1. Management must recognize that improvement is needed.

2. Everyone in the organization must receive team training.

3. Everyone in the organization must receive SPC training.

4. Everyone in the organization should be committed to improvement.

5. Employees must be allowed true empowerment.

6. Employees must be provided with JIT training. As the need arises they must be provided the appropriate training.

7. The successes must be publicized.

8. Risk-taking must be allowed and, in some cases, encouraged.

9. Participation and application must be encouraged.

10. The team must be congratulated.

Section II: Sector-Specific Requirements—Chrysler, Ford, and GM

Section II is a part of the QS-9000 document auditable by third-party registrars and it contains 13 "shalls." Their distribution is divided into three parts, in the following areas: Production Part Approval Process (1 shall), Continuous Improvement (6 shalls), and Manufacturing Capabilities (6 shalls).

Production Part Approval Process

General—1.1. The supplier must use the PPAP manual whenever submitting a new or changed component or part to the automotive community (Chrysler, Ford, and GM 1995d). This includes, but is not limited to, anytime that

- A new part is designed
- A change occurs to an existing part
  —A major characteristic changes
- A process change occurs (how the part is made)
  —Where the part is manufactured
  —A material change occurs
  —New or different machinery is used to make the part

Engineering Change Validation—1.2. Within the requirements of the PPAP, the supplier has to verify the changes and that they are validated according to the procedure(s), that all tests and/or inspections are conducted as required, and that all documentation is properly filled out. There are slight differences between OEM's requirements, so the supplier should check with the customer first to identify the specific requirements.

Continuous Improvement

General—2.1. Three shalls are found in this subsection. The supplier must have a continuous improvement philosophy that is fully deployed throughout the organization—including the front office, the shop floor, the chief executive, and the janitor. Areas of documented improvements must include quality, service, and price as a starting point. Also, action plans for continuous improvement must be identified for those areas that the customer feels are the most important.

The automotive industry emphasizes the use of variables data whenever possible in looking for continuous improvement opportunities. However, if variables data are not used, then attribute data are to be used in the continuous improvement effort and documented advancements will need to be demonstrated.

Note 1: This note refers to areas that can be measured using variables data. Reduction of variation around the identified target value is needed to optimize the part characteristics or process parameters.

Note 2: A recommendation is made here that this improvement should not be limited to just the shop floor. As Peters (1992) pointed out, an excellent company does not develop by doing one thing a thousand percent better, but by doing a thousand things one percent better each. Thus, documented improvements need to be shown in all areas.

- Engineering parameters: number of changes, cycle time, quote time, and so on
- Marketing parameters: time to quote, call backs, and so on
- Office operations: scheduling, identification of internal customers and their satisfaction, processing of jobs, how well work is done
- Financial management: report cycle time, accuracy, distribution of reports

- Human relations: recruitment practices, retention, turnover, handling complaints
- Training: delivery methods, development time and quality, number and types of training, who gets trained and why
- Custodial services: cleanliness of the facilities and grounds, cycle time in cleaning

When looking for nonmanufacturing improvement opportunities, there are two basic parameters that may be considered: the time that it takes to do something, and how well the work is being done. Looking at these two areas can lead to big improvements in satisfying not only external customers but also internal customers, thus allowing the operations to run more smoothly.

Quality and Productivity Improvements—2.2. The supplier must identify improvement projects in the areas of quality and productivity. An example list is presented, but is limited to the shop floor. The supplier may well be asked to show documentation on what has or is being planned, how they are doing, and what has been accomplished to date. One method of satisfying these requirements in a systematic format is the Ford QOS method. The QOS is a standardized management program that maximizes performance through a total system approach for customer satisfaction. It focuses on effective communication throughout the organization and uses standard tools and methodologies for implementing incremental and breakthrough improvements in both manufacturing and nonmanufacturing applications.

Techniques for Continuous Improvement—2.3. Fourteen specific tools and methodologies are identified that the supplier must not only know about but must also be using, as appropriate, in its continuous improvement efforts. These tools include

- Capability indices (C_p, C_{pk}, P_{pk})
- Control charts (variables, attributes)

Cumulative sum charting (cusum)
- Design of experiments (DOE)
  —Classical
  —Taguchi
  —Other techniques developed by Dorian Shainin
- Evolutionary operation of processes (EVOP)
- Theory of constraints
- Mistake proofing
- Analysis of ergonomics
- Overall equipment effectiveness
- Cost of quality
  —Prevention
  —Appraisal
  —Internal failures
  —External failures
- Parts per million (PPM) analysis
- Value analysis
- Problem solving
  —Chrysler uses a 7D
  —Ford uses an 8D or team-oriented problem-solving approach
  —GM has a problem reporting and resolution procedure (GM 1995)
- Benchmarking
  Be cautious of looking only at the large picture here. Many microprocesses can be benchmarked as well. Be cautious also about benchmarking only within a certain industry. Sometimes the best innovations come from outside the current paradigms in the field.

Manufacturing Capabilities

Facilities, Equipment, and Process Planning and Effectiveness—3.1. In addition to the requirements for using a cross-functional team called out in the APQP manual (Chrysler, Ford, and GM 1995a), the supplier must also use this team approach to develop facilities, processes, and equipment plans. How efficient and effective the existing and future operations are must be identified. This allows for improvement opportunities as identified in the preceding component.

Mistake Proofing—3.2. At all phases of APQP or production, mistake proofing must be used. This is true whenever a problem or potential problem exists. Other terms used for this technique are sometimes referred to as *poke-yoke, error proofing, idiot proofing, foolproof design,* and so on. The terms *idiot proofing* and *foolproof design* are rarely used today as they are very demeaning to the operator who may have no control over the system and yet has been designated to produce the part.

Tool Design and Fabrication—3.3. Two "shalls" are identified here. Tool and gauge design, fabrication, and full dimensional inspection is the responsibility of the supplier and must be given proper technical assistance even if this work is subcontracted. Also, customer-owned tools and equipment must be permanently and visibly marked so that the owner is clearly identified.

Tooling Management—3.4. Self-explanatory.

Section III: Customer-Specific Requirements

This section was changed drastically in the 1995 edition of the QS-9000 document. There are five additions, one correction, and two updates from the original version. Also, this section is now third-party auditable, as clarified by the February 9, 1996 issue of the *IASG Sanctioned QS-9000 Interpretations* (IASG 1996). Most of the general requirements are covered in Sections I and II, and this section simply clarifies what specific customers require of their suppliers. With this said, though, each of the Big Three has a number of requirements that suppliers are expected to follow that are not called out specifically in Sections I and II. These requirements are areas in which harmonization was not achieved and each company continues to conduct business in its own way. Some may even feel that the way they do business leads to a competitive advantage over the others.

In Section III, the rule of the word *shall* is expanded to other words as well (such as *must, will, required,* and so on). This section should be read very carefully to ensure that the supplier is complying to the customer's requirements, as indicated in certain documents and/or measurement controls and/or records. A number of company-specific reference manuals are mentioned in this section, and the supplier is expected to have each of these in its possession, available to anyone in the company that needs them. This fact will be verified by the third-party registrar under document control, Element 4.5.1.

To locate these documents, Ford and GM suppliers should call the appropriate contact given in the QS-9000 manual, pages 68 and 70 respectively. Chrysler suppliers should contact their own buyers.

Chrysler-Specific Requirements

Parts Identified with Symbols. Chrysler uses three special symbols to indicate items on blueprints that need to be controlled in the manufacturing process. Each symbol has specific requirements as to what is to be done with the part characteristics with which the symbol is associated.

1. *The shield.* This symbol is Chrysler's identification of safety and/or other important characteristics that are to receive special attention by the suppliers to meet the requirements of

Chrysler or government regulations. Chrysler has published a manual titled *Shields—Critical Characteristics Guidelines* (Chrysler 1994b) and expects suppliers to use it.

2. *The diamond.* This symbol (or the letter D) is used by Chrysler to identify nonregulatory critical characteristics. Special attention is to be given to these items during production to ensure that they especially meet all engineering specifications and design intent.

3. *The pentagon.* Whenever a special characteristic is identified, then the pentagon (or the letter *P*) is used for identification. Chrysler has a special manual to explain the use of this symbol; the manual should be added to the supplier's collection of customer's manuals. The *Pentagon—Critical Verification Symbol Guidelines* (Chrysler 1994a) is not mentioned in Chrysler's bibliography, but is still needed.

Significant Characteristics. This designation is left up to the supplier and is to be used on any part/tooling characteristic that needs special attention while the part is in the hands of the supplier. The only shall in this element indicates that these significant characteristics are to be addressed in the supplier's control plan.

Annual Layout. Chrysler requires an annual layout on all parts that the supplier ships.

Internal Quality Audits. The QS-9000 document requires that auditing be conducted periodically to remain in compliance with the standard. Chrysler also requires that an annual internal quality system audit be conducted. This does not relate to third-party registration and could be conducted by anyone chosen by the supplier. However, auditing must be conducted by individuals that have no vested interest in the area that they audit. Thus, a supervisor cannot audit her or his own department as part of this annual requirement. Records will be maintained.

Design Validation/Production Verification. An annual design valida-
tion/production verification check must be conducted on all new or
carryover parts. One of the manuals listed in Chrysler's bibliography deals with this requirement.

Corrective Action Plan. Chrysler uses a 7D approach to address
nonconformances within its system (not the same as Ford's 8D).
The reporting format is quite explicit in the QS-9000 document.

Packaging, Shipping, and Labeling. Two manuals should be followed in this area. Neither is listed in the bibliography, but are help-
ful at each production point in the supplier's system. The two
manuals are *Packaging and Shipping Instructions Manual* (Chrysler
n.d.) and *Shipping/Parts Identification Label Standards Manual*
(Chrysler n.d.).

Process Sign-Off. Chrysler is trying to ensure that each supplier has
a systematic and sequential review of all processes in the supplier's
system. This is not limited to shop-floor activities, but the entire
system. During new product development, this responsibility
should lie in the hands of the advanced quality planning team.

*Lot Acceptance Sampling Table, Product Characteristic Classifi-
cation and Product Qualification Table.* This item is new in the second addition, however, it is self-explanatory.

Chrysler Bibliography. Seven manuals (sometime referred to as the
Blue Dot series) are available for suppliers working with Chrysler.
Each of these documents should be available at each of the supplier's locations. The manuals provide valuable information in dealing with Chrysler's requirements.

Ford-Specific Requirements

Of the Big Three, Ford lists the most specific items that it wants its
suppliers to follow. Ford also expands the mandatory requirements
beyond *shall* to include *must, will,* and *is required.*

Of special interest is that Ford has gone through some major managerial and structural changes in recent months and the people who participated in these changes are no longer with the company. Readers should start by contacting the appropriate office identified on page 68 of the QS-9000 manual. The other source of information is Supplier Technical Assistance (STA). STA replaced Supplier Quality Engineering (SQE), which no longer exists.

Control Item (Inverted Delta) Parts. The inverted delta symbol (called *delta* for short) is used in conjunction with the part number any time safety or governmental regulations must be followed. The delta symbol indicates that something about the function of that part must be monitored and controlled with very special care. Usually, Ford Product Engineering will identify the delta items. However, the supplier may choose to treat other parts with this same care. Ford's partner, Mazda, uses the symbols of "A" and "AR" to indicate safety or government regulations.

Control Plans and FMEAs. There are three mandatory requirements in this element. Control plans and FMEAs are required by all of the Big Three. Ford additionally requires customer sign-off when inverted delta items are involved. In such cases, these documents must be approved by both the design and quality engineers working for Ford. This required sign-off extends also to any revisions to these documents. This can become a challenge to the supplier, as these documents are called *living documents* and are to be maintained in some cases on a daily basis and/or by the people on the shop floor doing the work.

A *control plan* is a document that describes the actions that are required at each phase of the process, including receiving, in-process, and outgoing, as well as periodic requirements to ensure that all process outputs will be in a state of control. During normal production runs, the control plan provides the process monitoring and control methods that will be used to control characteristics.

Remember that the control plan must be responsive to all changes in the process condition.

An FMEA maximizes the satisfaction of the customer by eliminating and/or reducing known or potential problems from the process. For a more detailed discussion see Stamatis (1995), SAE (1994), Chrysler, Ford, and GM (1995c), and Ford (1993b).

The third requirement has to do with design FMEAs. Stamatis (1995) defines a *design FMEA* as a disciplined analysis/method of identifying potential or known failure modes and providing follow-up and corrective actions before the first production run. A design FMEA usually is accomplished through a series of steps to include components, subsystems, and/or systems. The design FMEA is an evolutionary process involving the application of various technologies and methods to produce an effective design output. This result will be used as an input for the process or assembly and/or the service FMEA.

A number of Big Three suppliers are trying to skirt the issue of identifying the design product for the automotive industry by applying for ISO 9002 or QS-9000 without including Section 4.4. This practice is being investigated very seriously by the Big Three. Some companies that have already done this may soon find themselves having to recall the registrars at added costs to reevaluate their system using ISO 9001 Clause 4.4, Design Control. Readers are strongly encouraged to review the design control section (4.4) to determine whether or not they are responsible for design.

Shipping Container Label. Suppliers must pay special attention to shipping labels if the parts are designated as delta parts; the delta symbol must also be on the label. Ford publishes guideline manuals for how to label the product shipped into its plants.

Equipment Standard Parts. Sometimes a governmental agency identifies a part as special because of public safety issues. These equipment standard parts are to be certified by Ford's suppliers to conform to all requirements that may be placed on the function and fit of the part. Ford is officially notifying the suppliers that they (not Ford) will be held responsible and accountable to the government if anything goes wrong with the parts.

Critical Characteristics. Suppliers should carefully monitor specific aspects of a part or the process that produced the part. A delta symbol is again used to indicate that these characteristics or process parameters are to be given specific handling or monitoring.

Setup Verification. Suppliers are required to use statistical confirmation that machines meet desired parameters for production, according to the control plan and FMEA. This requirement applies to any part identified as having critical (delta symbol) or significant (Ford's other special designation) characteristics, as identified in the control plan.

Control Item Fasteners. When a part uses fasteners that are identified as delta items due to how the fastener works, then the supplier must give special attention to the following three areas.

1. *Material Analysis—Heat-Treated Parts.* Most metal is initially identified by a heat number given to it by the producing mill. When fasteners are made and then hardened using heat-treating methods, samples of the metal must be tested to specific requirements. Documentation is required to show any results of testing done on the metal at various stages of this overall process and records showing all relationships back to the original mill's heat number are to be kept.

2. *Material Analysis—Non–Heat-Treated Parts.* All metal that does not go through the hardening process must be visually checked for the mill heat number and that the number agrees with all paperwork. A test is required to confirm the paperwork that came with the material.

3. *Lot Traceability.* Some form of lot traceability is required in all cases dealing with a delta-identified part or process. Special care is required to maintain this process. If a recall ever occurs, these records will more than pay for themselves by identifying what needs to be done during the investigation.

Heat Treating. For specific instances dealing with heat treating, two specific Ford specifications are called out for process control. These documents are unique to Ford and have requirements in how heat treating is conducted.

The third "must" requires that all suppliers using heat-treated parts be assessed to the Ford Heat Treat System Survey Guidelines. If suppliers do not have the appropriate reference material, they are encouraged to contact the appropriate office within Ford, which is given on page 68 of the QS-9000 document. If that does not produce any results, then the supplier should to contact its STA, and if that fails, it is to conduct its own self-assessment.

Ford also requires heat treating to be controlled to prevent brittle parts.

Process Changes and Design Changes for Supplier-Responsible Designs. Control items, parts, and/or other specially designated designs must not be changed without prior approval by Ford Motor Company. A special form is available from Ford Purchasing to request changes to these parts if change is deemed necessary.

Supplier Modification of Control Item Requirements. Suppliers are encouraged to make improvements to products and services provided to Ford. Before any changes are actually implemented, however, appropriate approvals must be obtained.

Engineering Specification Test Performance Requirements. If a required test of a product fails to meet the design intent, the supplier must stop all shipments of product until the cause of the failure is identified and corrected. All affected production facilities must be notified immediately and suspect materials cannot be shipped until 100-percent inspection is conducted. If the cause of the failure cannot be determined, the supplier must contact Ford Production Engineering for further instructions.

System Design Specification. There is no specific requirement here, only a definition of what *system design specification* (SDS) is. The definition of SDS is "a compilation of performance metrics for a system or subsystem." These metrics could be used in developing a QOS within your company.

Ongoing Process Monitoring. This element references two tables within the QS-9000 document on pages 67 and 68. These tables are meant to be used as guidelines and are to be followed any time the product characteristic is not otherwise directed by an approved control plan. For more information in this area see Moura (1991), Brush (1988), and Meeker (1985).

1. *Qualifications of All Product Characteristics—Table A.* This table consists of two parts: Sample Size Recommendations for Product Qualification and Product Qualification. The first looks at how many parts need to be looked at or tested to ensure that the lot or shipment is good for production. Product Qualification gives guidelines identifying what to do if any nonconforming units (parts) are found in the lot or shipment.

    Sample Size Recommendations for Product Qualification: Lot sizes are to consist of eight hours' or one day's production, whichever is smaller. To start with, at least 200 parts must be checked to approve the lot. After 20 consecutive lots have been found to be totally good with no nonconforming parts, then the sample size can be reduced to 50 parts. However, if a nonconforming unit is found at any time thereafter, the lot must be 100-percent sorted and returned to a sample size of 200.

Product Qualification: When no nonconforming parts are found, accept the lot and continue to operate. If any nonconforming units are found, root causes must be found and corrective action taken.

Note that the word *nonconforming* is required to be used instead of the word *defect* (see Chapter 2). This has come about due to legal issues in North America where sampling plans have allowed a certain number of defects in the system. The legal profession has challenged this in court and won large settlements against the Big Three for not requiring 100-percent good parts all the time. Thus, today the requirements look at units not conforming to the intended specifications. Nonconforming does not mean that the part is totally unusable, only that it does not meet all the design parameters to the optimum conditions. For a more detailed discussion see Stamatis (1995, Chapter 1).

2. *Ongoing Process and Product Monitoring—Table B.* This graph looks at the use of variables data and the calculation of C_{pk}. Ford used a target value of 1.33 on the C_{pk} scale. This equals a total of eight standard deviations based on the process in question compared with the engineering specifications. By putting the engineering specifications on top (numerator) and dividing by six times the standard deviation (denominator), the numerical value of C_{pk} is calculated. It is expected that the ratio value be higher than 1.0 and preferably higher than 1.33.

Basically, if the C_{pk} for the process is less than 1.33, the output of the process must be inspected 100 percent of the time. If the C_{pk} for the process is 1.33 or greater, continue to run the process and ship the product. When samples are found to contain parts that are out of specification, special rules take effect. For a more detailed explanation on how to work with C_p and C_{pk} as well as the P_p and P_{pk}, see the *Statistical Process Control: Reference Manual* developed by Chrysler, Ford, and GM (1995f) and distributed by AIAG and Ford.

Prototype Part Quality Initiatives. During the prototype phase of a part's life, very little data are available to perform SPC well. However, Ford does require suppliers to collect data on the prototype parts and make some elementary data-based assumptions. The assumptions are product and experience dependent. The calculations are done during the prototype phase: percentage of inspection points that satisfy tolerance (PIST) and percent indices that are process capable (PIPC).

- PIST is a ratio of how many inspection points or characteristics actually meet the specifications over the total number of characteristics checked in that lot. This number gives a baseline to judge how well the supplier is doing and an even playing field for evaluating continuous improvement on future jobs as well as against other suppliers.

- PIPC is a ratio of how many C_{pk} characteristics are 1.33 or greater over the total number of characteristics being evaluated. This is not a true C_{pk} value because, more often than not, there usually are not enough data available. Ford is trying to get an initial picture of where the process is and where further work needs to be done either by Ford or the supplier.

QOS. Ford's suppliers are required to use the concepts and methodology of QOS. This system of total quality management uses a specific model designed to ensure both internal and external customer satisfaction. This process can be have a profound effect on the supplier's organization as levels of QOS are developed. A steering committee may meet once a month to evaluate how the entire process is running, but a number of smaller groups are expected to be working on problems and continuous improvement efforts at other times throughout the month.

The supplier will be evaluated on the effectiveness of its QOS through the *QOS Assessment & Rating Procedure* manual (Ford 1993a). Evaluations are currently performed by both STAs and/or Ford buyers. Either way, the supplier will be asked to present its monthly findings at a meeting in Dearborn, Michigan, or to run its normal monthly meeting with Ford representatives present in the supplier's organization. If the supplier needs QOS training, Ford is equipped to provide it (Chrysler, Ford, and GM 1994b).

Qualification and Acceptance Criteria for Materials. Control plans must be approved before parts are produced and shipped. Here, Ford identifies who the Ford contact is for such approvals. The contact, more often than not, is Ford Materials Engineering. This group will review and approve all supplier control plans and also maintain the engineering materials approved source list that is to be followed for any special required materials. If the supplier is unsure about who to contact in this group, Ford Purchasing will help find the right person to talk to.

Ford Bibliography. Seven specific Ford reference manuals are listed here, with the origination group named that developed the manual and the appropriate addresses where suppliers may obtain the manuals. Suppliers need these manuals in their quest for quality, at least as Ford has defined it. Suppliers should contact Ford buyers or STA to make sure that the requirements are current.

General Motors-Specific Requirements

General Procedures and Other Requirements. GM has a number of other requirements that must be followed by the supplier. Any supplier doing business with GM must have all 17 booklets or manuals identified by GM. All specific requirements for GM are delineated through the 17 publications without further explanation. It is imperative, however, that all suppliers verify the use of the latest version of these documents at least annually because they may change.

Even though all the references given on page 70–71 of the QS-9000 document are indeed required by GM, there are some special items that the suppliers ought to be more careful with.

1. Key characteristics designation system (GP-1805), which defines GM's approach to special characteristics.

2. Continuous improvement procedure (GP-8), which is required of all suppliers and replaces part certification procedure.

3. Run at rate (GP-9), which became a new requirement as of February 1995 and is required for all new parts. It requires physical verification that the production process is capable of producing quality products at quoted rates.

4. Evaluation and accreditation of supplier test facilities (GP-10), which states that third-party registration to QS-9000 in accordance with Appendix B will satisfy the GP-10 requirements for GM North American locations of laboratory facilities used by suppliers for inspection and testing of their own product for purposes of conformance to the specified requirements. Laboratories utilized for commercial laboratory services are excluded from this provision.

5. Early production containment procedure (GP-12), which became a new requirement as of February 1995 and is required of all parts requiring production approval.

Truck Manufacturers-Specific Requirements

The four truck manufactures that require the use of *Quality Systems Requirements: QS-9000* are identified. Each trucking company (like the Big Three) has additional individual requirements, and suppliers should contact the appropriate truck manufacturer's purchasing department for further instructions.

Appendixes and Other Back Matter

Appendix A: The Quality System Assessment Process

Close attention should be paid to this appendix because it outlines in three pages how suppliers should conduct the quality system assessment process. There are a number of "shalls" in this appendix, and the suppliers and registrars should follow these requirements to ensure that QS-9000 is fully implemented.

Alternative Methods for Verifying Supplier Conformance to Quality System Requirements. The manual lists two methods for verifying conformance to QS-9000, either by second-party (by way of customer representatives) assessments or by third-party (approved registrar) assessments. However, this is misleading for some suppliers. GM has already mandated that all its suppliers become third-party registered (Martin 1994). According to GM, the following is the most current information on GM's implementation plan and other company-specific details.

> As a current supplier to General Motors you will be required to be registered to the quality system requirements by a third party (quality system registrar) no later than December 31, 1997. Therefore, we recommend that you immediately begin working toward your third-party registration.

For your information, the following implementation dates apply to new suppliers to General Motors.

- Effective 1/1/95, GM began potential supplier audit based on the QSA manual.

- Effective 1/1/96, third-party registration to the quality system requirements will be required for all *new* suppliers.

Ford has announced that it will only conduct second-party assessments on an exception basis. Ford is committed to ISO 9000 via the QS-9000 requirements. The expected effective date is December 31, 1996.

Perhaps the most demanding schedule for implementation of QS-9000 is that of Chrysler. Chrysler, on January 11, 1995, announced the following (Stallkamp 1995):

> As a valued Chrysler supplier, you are expected to update your existing quality systems to meet the requirements of QS-9000. The success of QS-9000 will depend upon the commitment of key individuals such as yourself.

Furthermore, Chrysler announced the following.

- A self-assessment to QS-9000 must be completed by all suppliers before July 7, 1995. Only the results and general comments pages of the QSA (pp. 38–39) are to be sent to Chrysler. Instructions regarding the return of the self-assessment will be provided in the near future.

- All production and service part suppliers to Chrysler must be third-party registered to QS-9000 by July 31, 1997, willing to undergo second-party assessments as a regular part of their business.

This situation in turn will cause suppliers some problems, at least during the short term. There are simply not enough trained and qualified registrars available to conduct all the third-party assessments that need to be done. Thus the laws of supply and demand will dictate long waiting times and probably higher costs to get started in using QS-9000.

Suppliers that are trying to decide whether to use a registrar should consider these questions.

- Does one of your customers require third-party registration? If not, can you request a second-party assessment?

- When does the customer require third-party registration (even Ford and Chrysler will probably require it sooner or later)?

- Does the registrar have the available resources to service your organization in a timely manner? It is a simple fact that at this time and for the near term, there are not enough trained individuals available to the automotive industry to conduct third-party assessments.

- Have you performed a cost analysis between the registrar and/or a second-party assessment?

- What is the return on investment of using a third party at this time? The law of supply and demand will cause many suppliers grief due to few registrars and/or auditors combined with customer requirements to become registered.

- As one automotive supplier recently stated, are you willing to answer the six tough questions about QS-9000?

  —Do you have the time (and money) to implement QS-9000 correctly?

  —Will your corporate culture accept "quality systems" as outlined in QS-9000?

  —Will top management support the structure and system required to achieve and maintain QS-9000?

  —Will the systems add value?

  —Is the system simple and flexible enough to allow room for change?

  —Can you really implement the new changes?

Periodically customers may want to look over some of the data resulting from this entire process. This could be as simple as reviewing the audit report prepared by the audit team or taking a closer look at some of the documentation that needs to be completed as a result of complying with QS-9000. Several items need particular attention, because these items are most important if and when a customer asks questions due to a problem.

- The quality manual (level 1 documentation)
- The procedures (level 2 documentation)
- Documentation of self-assessment to the QS-9000 requirements using at least the information from the *Quality System Assessment* (Chrysler, Ford, and GM 1994b)
- Documentation of ongoing internal audit results

If a supplier finds it will be dealing with an accredited third-party registrar, the typical registration process should include the following:

- A contractual agreement (remember that the supplier should interview various registrars before entering into an agreement with any one)
- Quality manual review (manual preparation in accordance with ISO 10013)
- Preassessment/document review
- On-site assessment
- Corrective action closure (various registrars use different terms to identify major and minor actions; this must be addressed before registration)
- Registration (three years) and report
- Surveillance (six months)
- Reassessment cycle (three years)

A commonly asked question in larger organizations is: Does our division headquarters need to be registered as well? The answer, typically, is yes! The supplier needs to work with the registrar, preferably ahead of time, to determine all the details of how the process should work. You need to find a registrar that will fit in with the culture of your organization, be eager to help your company succeed, have experience in your field, be a recognized registrar worldwide, and be firm but have a fair (unbiased) attitude toward your company.

The Customer's Decision Process. Customers always have the option to review your quality systems. Generally this will be done by either verifying that the supplier has a valid certificate showing conformance to QS-9000 and/or reviewing the audit results report given to the supplier by the registrar. In some cases, however, the customer may wish to view additional information concerning the supplier's quality system. This may include, but is not limited to, the following:

- The four items mentioned previously

- A plan showing implementation timing and which approved registrar will be used (if the supplier is not already registered)

- Copies of the registrar's certificate showing that it is certified to conduct QS-9000 audits

After reviewing this information, the customer may choose (except for GM's date requirements) to accept the supplier's action plan and its intentions to become registered. Suppliers that do not meet these criteria will be dealt with on an individual basis.

The Big Three have stated that, generally, they will not subject suppliers to redundant audits if the supplier is QS-9000 certified and is shipping good parts. If, however, the supplier fails to meet these two criteria, the Big Three can require the supplier to meet their specific, individual needs.

In this section, two more items are mentioned. (1) Second-party audits are not the same as third-party registration to the QS-9000 requirements; and (2) OEM supplier ratings are outside the scope of QS-9000. GM has announced that its Target for Excellence (TFE) flags and plaques will be discontinued (Martin 1994).

A generic flowchart is shown on page 77 of the QS-9000 document showing the progression of steps a supplier should follow in achieving registration to QS-9000.

Appendix B: Code of Practice for Quality Systems Registrars
This appendix is for registrars that intend to conduct QS-9000 audits. There are 12 specific items with which the registrar must comply to be authorized to perform these audit for the automotive industry. The supplier should carefully select a registrar and verify that the registrar is indeed complying with and has signed this code of practice. Any supplier that is registered to QS-9000 by a registrar not following these practices is in danger of losing its registration and will have to begin the registration process again with a new registrar.

1. Only certain national accredited bodies have adopted the QS-9000 requirements. For a current list, contact ASQC (800-248-1946) or look at the latest version of the *IASG Sanctioned QS-9000 Interpretations.* The list is growing, and it is imperative for the supplier about to be immersed in QS-9000 implementation to find an authorized accreditation body as well as registrar.

2. QS-9000 has become a contractual requirement for all production and service parts suppliers to the Big Three and trucking manufacturers. The registrar must follow the QS-9000 requirements.

3. Besides the 244 "shalls" in Sections I and II, registrars can audit other customer requirements relating to elements of the supplier's quality system implementation. Thus, copies of any reference manuals cited anywhere in the QS-9000 document should be on file as applicable to the customer base and used in developing the supplier's quality system.

4. During the audit, registrars should look at both effective implementation of the QS-9000 requirements as well as the effectiveness in practice.

5. All accreditation bodies and ISO guidelines are to be followed when registrars conduct their business and perform their audits, based on EN 45012, *General Criteria for Certification Bodies Operating Quality System Certification,* dated May 10, 1994.

6. Registrars must review three minimum areas (as identified in this item). The supplier will be required to show that these items are accurate and up-to-date. This could become a real challenge for the supplier, especially in the area of customer complaints because the Big Three are still working on their systems to notify suppliers of problems. A supplier may be advised to start a proactive approach to ensure that all complaints are logged and that action can then be taken to attempt a resolution.

7. A major audit of each manufacturing location must be conducted every three years. In addition to this requirement, six-month surveillance audits are to be performed to ensure that everything is being maintained.

8. The registrar must provide a complete audit report to the supplier within 45 days of the audit. The audit is to contain identified areas for improvement, but the registrar is not allowed to make recommendations about what specific improvements to make. Registrar companies are thus not allowed to be in the consulting business. This may seem to suppliers that are told something is wrong but are not told how to fix it, but registrars must be independent of both the Big Three and the supplier as far as reporting lines are established.

9. Consultants are not acceptable as registrars. Only fully approved registrars are allowed to grant a registration. The reporting lines of individuals working for registrars and consultants are very clearly set. Any consultant or individual

who claims to have some inside knowledge and/or guarantee that he or she can achieve registration for a company should be looked at with *great* caution. Consultants can play an important role in assisting in the pursuit of registration. The supplier, however, should be wary of claims made versus promises kept.

10. The registrar is required to provide an audit team with the appropriate training and certifications to conduct not only ISO 9000 audits, but also QS-9000 audits. Thus everyone on the team must be an approved auditor for ISO 9000, and the majority of team members must have a certificate of completion of QS-9000 training. At the present time, the only training approved for QS-9000 is authorized through the AIAG.

11. Consultants hired by the supplier are not allowed to participate in an audit conducted by a registrar organization. The only role a consultant could play is that of an observer during the actual audit.

12. One of the basic requirements that the registrar must follow in the audit is the manual called the *Quality System Assessment* (Chrysler, Ford, and GM 1994a). This document gives a starting point to the checklist that the registrar will develop and use during the audit. Registrations are not to be granted if any open major or minor nonconformances are found. The supplier must close all open issues before registration to QS-9000 is granted.

When a supplier has successfully completed all requirements for QS-9000 registration, the registrar will provide to the supplier a certificate indicating compliance to QS-9000 and the appropriate ISO 9000 series document. Once QS-9000 is completed, the supplier is automatically in compliance with ISO 9000. But the reverse is not true: Just because ISO 9000 registration has been achieved,

QS-9000 has not. There are still more than 100 other requirements listed in the QS-9000 that must be additionally audited.

Instructions to Suppliers Concerning Third-Party Registration. Suppliers are responsible for selecting registrars that are in compliance with the code of practice.

Appendix C: Special Characteristics and Symbols of QS-9000

The Big Three have not yet harmonized everything in the quality arena. They designate special characteristics and symbols differently in OEM manuals, drawings, and other related paperwork. For the specific designations, see page 82 of the QS-9000 document.

Appendix D: Local Equivalents for ISO 9001 and ISO 9002 Specifications

This is a matrix of documents equivalent to the ISO 9000 series in various countries around the world. Any of these documents can be used for the italicized portions of the QS-9000 document. However, there are more than 100 additional requirements of the automotive industry that go beyond the ISO 9001 requirements.

Appendix E: Acronyms and Their Meanings

The U.S. automotive industry is blessed with a large vocabulary of acronyms. It is not uncommon for engineers to talk in complete sentences using only specific jargon and acronyms; for example, "MSA, SPC, PPAP, FMEA, and APQP training will all count for the ASQC CQE, CRE, and/or CQA requirement to earn 18 RUs every three years." This means, "Measurement system analysis, statistical process control, production part approval process, failure mode and effects analysis, and advanced product quality planning training will all count for the ASQC certified quality engineer, certified reliability engineer, and/or certified quality auditor requirement to earn 18 recertification units every three years."

This combination of jargon and acronyms causes many communication problems for those dealing with each of the Big Three because a number of these acronyms are different for each one of them. A list from one of the Big Three firms has 54 pages of acronyms for the supplier quality part of the business (Ford 1994a). It is reported that this list is less than 50 percent of what is used. The list incorporated with the QS-9000 document has 41 items that are common between the companies.

Of special interest is the ISO acronym itself: The true name is the International Organization for Standardization, and not what most Americans believe as the International Standards Organization.

Appendix F: Change Summary

This appendix, new in the 1995 edition, provides QS-9000 document readers with the significant changes between the first and second editions. There are 50 changes in total (see Chapter 1 for a detailed list of the changes). They include additions, updates, corrections, clarifications, modifications, and deletions.

Appendix G: November 21, 1994 QS-9000 Accreditation Body Implementation Requirements

This appendix, new in the 1995 edition, provides basic information needed to implement the QS-9000 requirements. There are 15 minimum requirements for registrars, five for accreditation bodies, and four for automotive companies.

Appendix H: Survey Audit Days Table

This appendix, new in the 1995 edition, helps readers predict how long the initial and ongoing audits should take for a given organization. The criteria for the minimum length is based on the number of employees in the organization. This table has been revised, and the new information can be found in the IASG-sanctioned interpretations dated November 9, 1995 (IASG 1995).

Glossary

There are 37 terms defined in this glossary, which are defined relative to practices and procedures used by the automotive industry.

The term *consulting* has definite overtones and is meant to distinguish between who is qualified to conduct third-party audits and who is not. The desire is that anyone doing consulting work should not be allowed to conduct third-party audits under QS-9000. However, they may be allowed to conduct ISO 9000 audits.

Contact Information

The last page of the QS-9000 document lists the names of the OEM Task Force members who can be contacted for further information.

References

ANSI/ISO/ASQC. 1995. ANSI/ISO/ASQC Q10013-1995, *Guidelines for developing quality manuals.* Milwaukee, Wis.: ASQC.

Brush, G. G. 1988. *Volume 12: How to choose the proper sample size.* Milwaukee, Wis.: ASQC Quality Press.

Chrysler Corporation. n.d. *Packaging and shipping instructions manual.* Auburn Hills, Mich.: Supplier Quality Office, Chrysler Corporation.

Chrysler Corporation. n.d. *Shipping/parts identification label standards manual.* Auburn Hills, Mich.: Supplier Quality Office, Chrysler Corporation.

Chrysler Corporation. 1994a. *The pentagon—Critical verification symbol guidelines.* Auburn Hills, Mich.: Corporate Quality Office, Chrysler Corporation.

Chrysler Corporation. 1994b. *Shields—Critical characteristics guidelines.* Auburn Hills, Mich.: Corporate Quality Office, Chrysler Corporation.

Chrysler Corporation, Ford Motor Company, and General Motors Corporation. 1994a. *Quality system assessment.* Southfield, Mich.: Chrysler Corporation, Ford Motor Company, and General Motors Corporation.

———. 1994b. *Quality system assessment training.* Southfield, Mich.: Chrysler Corporation, Ford Motor Company, and General Motors Corporation.

———. 1994c. *Quality system requirements: QS-9000.* Southfield, Mich.: Chrysler Corporation, Ford Motor Company, and General Motors Corporation.

———. 1995a. *Advanced product quality planning and control plan: Reference manual.* Southfield, Mich.: Chrysler Corporation, Ford Motor Company, and General Motors Corporation.

———. 1995b. *Measurement systems analysis: Reference manual.* Southfield, Mich.: Chrysler Corporation, Ford Motor Company, and General Motors Corporation.

———. 1995c. *Potential failure mode and effects analysis: Reference manual.* Southfield, Mich.: Chrysler Corporation, Ford Motor Company, and General Motors Corporation.

———. 1995d. *Production part approval process.* Southfield, Mich.: Chrysler Corporation, Ford Motor Company, and General Motors Corporation.

———. 1995e. *Quality system requirements: QS-9000.* Southfield, Mich.: Chrysler Corporation, Ford Motor Company, and General Motors Corporation.

———. 1995f. *Statistical process control: Reference manual.* Southfield, Mich.: Chrysler Corporation, Ford Motor Company, and General Motors Corporation.

Cvercko, S., J. Antonelli, and J. Steele. 1992. *Ford instructional systems design process*. Dearborn, Mich.: Instructional Methods Section, Ford Motor Company.

Ford Motor Company. 1990. *Planning for quality*. Dearborn, Mich.: Total Quality Excellence and Systems Management, Corporate Quality Office, Ford Motor Company.

———. 1993a. *QOS assessment & rating procedure*. Farmington Hills, Mich.: Ford Motor Company Quality Publication.

———. 1993b. *Failure mode and effect analysis: Handbook*. Dearborn, Mich.: Engineering Material and Standards, Technical Affairs, Ford Motor Company.

———. 1994a. *Acronym list*. Dearborn, Mich.: Supplier Quality Engineering, NAAO Vehicle Operations, Ford Motor Company.

———. 1994b. *Quality operating system*. Dearborn, Mich.: Supplier Quality Engineering, Ford Motor Company.

General Motors Corporation. 1995. *Problem reporting and resolution procedure*. City, Mich.: General Motor Corporation.

Hagenlocker, E. E. 1994. Ford automotive operations correspondence, 2 December. City, Mich.: Ford Motor Company.

International Automotive Sector Group. 1995. *IASG sanctioned QS-9000 interpretations*, 9 November. N.p.: International Automotive Sector Group.

———. 1996. *IASG sanctioned QS-9000 interpretations*, 9 February. N.p.: International Automotive Sector Group.

Martin, J. 1994. *Supplier communications*. Bulletin no. 94N198, 7 October. Detroit, Mich.: General Motors North American Operations.

Meeker, W. Q., and G. J. Hahn. 1985. *Volume 10: How to plan an accelerated life test*. Milwaukee, Wis.: ASQC Quality Press.

Moura, E. C. 1991. *Volume 15: How to determine sample size and estimate failure rate in life testing.* Milwaukee, Wis.: ASQC Quality Press.

Peters, T. 1992. *Liberation management.* New York: Alfred A. Knopf.

Philo, H. M., and H. M. Philo Jr. 1993–1994. *Lawyers desk reference.* 8th ed, 3 vols. New York: Clark, Boardman, Callaghan.

SAE. 1994. *Potential failure mode and effects analysis in design and potential failure mode and effects analysis is manufacturing and assembly processes: Process manual.* Surface Vehicle Recommended Practice SAE J 1739. Warrendale, Penn.: The Engineering Society for Advanced Mobility Land Sea Air and Space.

Stallkamp, T. T. 1995. Supplier communication, 11 January. Highland Park, Mich.: Chrysler Corporation.

Stamatis, D. H. 1995. *Failure mode and effect analysis: FMEA from theory to execution.* Milwaukee, Wis.: ASQC Quality Press.

CHAPTER 5

Third-Party Assessments

This chapter will explain the place of third-party assessment in the context of quality management systems and give some examples of the methods used by the various certification bodies. Limited consideration will also be given to the international scene with regard to third-party assessments.

Overview

A third-party assessment is one that is undertaken by an independent body to establish the extent to which an organization meets the requirements of an applicable standard or set of regulations. This approach to verification is totally foreign to the automotive industry, as most of the compliance to individual standards has been performed by the customer (second-party audit).

Third-party assessment bodies can be used to assess against any required standard. This chapter, however, concentrates on the assessment of a quality system such as described in the ISO 9000 series. The differences between ISO 9000 and QS-9000 are in the content, rather than the method, of the audit.

For both the ISO 9000 and QS-9000, the independent auditing body—the certification body or registrar—issues a certificate of registration, indicating acceptance of the organization as "a company of assessed capability," or something similar. This certification is issued after a review of the quality system and a physical audit of the organization. A typical certification process is shown in Figure 5.1.

The original certification takes approximately 10–24 months (including preparation time). After the certification is achieved, the certification body will visit the assessed organization once or twice a year for surveillance purposes and every three years for a major recertification assessment. The cycle of the surveillance and recertification is dependent upon the policy of the registrar and the agreement of the customer. For instance, the cycle for QS-9000 is surveillance every six months and recertification every three years.

Certification bodies are normally paid by the company that they assess, and they have no other association, including consulting services, with the assessed body. This is to ensure that the assessment is carried out without any bias.

Once this certification is issued, it bears witness to the world that the assessed organization complies with all of the requirements of the applicable standard. Certification does not guarantee product and/or service quality. It guarantees only the presence of a quality system.

Third-party assessment has been a common feature of commerce in the United Kingdom for many centuries. For example, the use of hallmarks began in 1140 A.D. As systems became available it was inevitable that third-party certification would be accepted not only in the United Kingdom but all over the world. Currently, there are about 18,000 companies in the United Kingdom and about 12,000 companies in the United States registered to ISO 9001 or ISO 9002, and the numbers are increasing at an exponential pace (Murrow 1996).

In the United States, third-party registration is also commonplace. For instance, the seal of approval from an accounting firm in an annual report is a form of third-party registration. The college

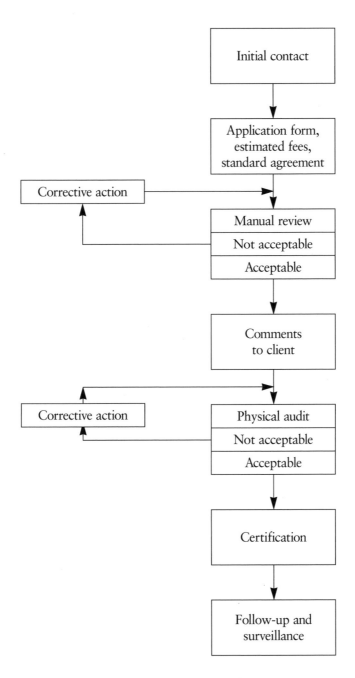

Figure 5.1. A generic ISO 9000 and QS-9000 certification process.

entrance exams (SAT, ACT) and professional/graduate entrance exams (GRE, GMAT, LSAT, and so on) are also a form of third-party registration.

Many of the countries that have accepted the ISO 9000 series standards look to the United Kingdom for advice and assistance on the implementation of the standards because it has the most experience in the area. This can be seen in countries where no system is yet established—individual companies turn to U.K. certification bodies for assessment. This is changing, however, as more countries provide certification. In the United States, for the latest information about registrars, contact RAB.

The System in the United States

Until recently, U.S. companies relied on quality system registration firms in Europe and Canada to register their quality systems. Today, the number of U.S.-based organizations offering consulting services, assessment, and/or quality system registration is growing rapidly.

One of the reasons for this growth is that in 1989 the Registrar Accreditation Board (RAB) was established as an affiliate of ASQC to develop a program to evaluate the quality of services offered by registrars. RAB issued its first approval in March 1991, and several more firms have been approved since then. RAB and the American National Standards Institute (ANSI) agreed to form a joint U.S. program in December 1991. In February 1992, RAB announced the establishment of an ISO 9000 auditor and lead auditor certification program. In addition to these certification programs, RAB is seeking mutual recognition from the EU Council. Preliminary negotiations began on October 20, 1992, and are still in progress as of this writing.

In the meantime, the degree of interest and pressure felt by U.S. manufacturers to seek registration currently varies significantly by industry. In many of the high-tech or high-risk product areas, where product reliability is crucial, the market pressure on U.S. manufacturers to seek registration is likely to be considerable.

The System in the World at Large

Many countries (93) around the world have now adopted the ISO 9000 series standards into their own national system. Of special interest is the European Union, which has adopted the standards as Euronormes (EN) 29000 to 29004. The tendency appears to be toward a worldwide recognition of the value of complying with the ISO quality system standards and continued progress toward third-party registration as being a reliable demonstration of compliance.

Most of the world has adopted the British system with the exception that each country has its own equivalent of the UKAS. It is not uncommon to find that most of the governing bodies in individual countries are controlled by a governmental agency.

Assessment Methods

The assessment is performed by a registrar. A registrar is an organization, not a person. However, the actual assessment is conducted by qualified (certified) auditors and lead auditors under the auspices of the registrar. A single person is not likely to become a registrar because registration decisions must be made by people other than those who conduct the audit. Each registrar must include a means for providing the overseeing of its operations—possibly a difficult task for a single-person organization (Bureau of Business Practice 1992). Each certification body has its own method of assessment and certification; however, all of them have some common ground, which will be the focus of this section.

The events of the certification procedure are as follows.

1. *Initial contact from the organization to the registrar.* General information is exchanged and appointments are set for the preassessment meeting.

2. *Preassessment visit.* Here either a questionnaire or an actual visit takes place to establish the amount of work needed.

3. *Quotation from the registrar.* A formal quote for the certification and surveillance services is given to the organization.

4. *Acceptance of the quote.* The organization signs the quote or a legal contract to accept the certification and surveillance services, as well as the price.

5. *Registrar asks for the quality system.* The quality system—sometimes called *documented system* or *desk audit*—is reviewed. This review assesses the system of the company as compared to the specific ISO standard to which the company is seeking certification. The purpose of this preaudit is to identify any omissions, ambiguities, or major nonconformities before the actual compliance audit.

6. *Compliance audit requested.* When the quality system is accepted, a request for the compliance audit is made.

7. *Compliance audit scheduled.* The compliance audit is generally undertaken with a team of auditors (assessors). The team is made up of one lead auditor and three to four auditors. The time allotted is usually no more than five days. A typical audit has the following elements.
   - Opening meeting
   - Audit
   - Closing meeting

8A. *Certification issued.* If everything goes well and no nonconformities have been found, then certification is issued. The actual certificate is issued four to eight weeks after the assessment. Although the actual certificate is not in the possession of the organization, the organization is officially certified as of the end of the audit.

8B. *Certification denied.* The denial may be of two forms, due to either minor noncompliances or major noncompliances. In either case, the organization might be reassessed when the noncompliances have been corrected.

Any nonconformity found must be recorded and its effect assessed by the lead auditor. Some registrars have a guidance procedure to assist in the ultimate decision.

A *major noncompliance* is the absence or the complete breakdown of a required element of the system. A required element is any of the subsections of Section 4 of the applicable standard. Sometimes, the terminology of *major noncompliance* is used interchangeably with *serious noncompliance* or *hold point.*

A *minor noncompliance* is an isolated failure to comply with specified requirements. A single minor noncompliance would not normally be a cause to fail the registration. However, a series of related minor nonconformities, in the judgment of the lead auditor, will more often than not constitute a breakdown of a procedure and/or the system. At this point, all related minor nonconformities are classified as major.

9. *Surveillance.* The registrars have the right to decertify an organization that fails to maintain an adequate standard. The ongoing program of making sure that the organization keeps up with the system will be described in the next section.

10. *Appeals.* If there is a conflict, the registrar usually has procedures that will define the appeals process. The process is generally as follows:

If during the audit an auditor does not conduct him- or herself in a professional manner or some other complaint is justified by the organization being audited, the audited organization has the right of appeal to the registrar. The actual process will depend on the specific registrar.

At that point, the registrar will investigate the complaint *with a person independent of the complaint.* If the registrar is unable to satisfy the customer, the customer has the right to complain to the certification body. At this stage, the certification body may review the complaint by asking for additional information and/or reissue an audit. In any case, the certification body has the ultimate decision. No more appeals are allowed.

Surveillance

To receive certification from a registrar is not the end point. Rather, it is the beginning of a commitment to a quality system that needs monitoring to ensure continued compliance with the standard. The actual monitoring varies from registrar to registrar; however, there are some common points.

All registrars have some kind of monitoring system. Some have a system of regular, unannounced audits; others have a reassessment at regular intervals (three years is a common interval) with either one or two supported audits annually.

Because one of the objectives of the certification is to ensure confidence in the system, the idea of the surveillance is to make sure that the effectiveness of the system will be continued for the assessed organization. A typical surveillance may cover the following:

- Check for maintenance of the internal audit program and appropriate corrective action.

- Check customer complaints and their follow-up.
- Check for satisfactory completion of all corrective actions agreed upon at the previous audit (internal or third-party).
- Sample check aspects of the quality system, possibly guided by recorded nonconformities from the last audit.
- Check appropriate use of the registrar's logo.
- Check for follow-up on all nonconformance items.
- Check whether the internal audits are utilized by top management for continual improvement purposes.

References

Bureau of Business Practice. 1992. *Profile of ISO 9000*. Needham Heights, Mass.: Allyn and Bacon.

Murrow, Mark. 1996. *ISO 9000 and QS-9000 survey*. Fairfax, Va.: Irwin Professional Publishing.

CHAPTER 6

Implementation Strategy for ISO 9000 Series Standards and QS-9000

This chapter addresses the reasons for and methods of evaluating the organization as well as the process of preparing the organization for the implementation of ISO 9000. Specifically, the issue of needs assessment and the mechanics of the implementation process in all levels of the organization will be presented.

The specific customer requirements of the QS-9000 system will not be covered because at this stage of the quality revolution in the United States, most, if not all, of the automotive suppliers are quite familiar with the techniques and procedures that are required for doing business with the major automobile manufacturers—Chrysler, Ford, and GM.

Needs Assessment

The needs of an organization and its employees are not static; they undergo changes over time. Therefore, it is important that management review itself. The forces for organizational change are many and constantly occurring as a result of changes in employee and/or corporate expectations, technology, knowledge, and a variety of social patterns.

To adequately assess the perceived needs of a system, representative segments of the corporate culture must be involved. By seeking information from the representative groups, the management can be more responsive to the wishes and real needs of the employees and the organization as a whole. The identification of needs involves a discrepancy analysis (gap analysis, needs analysis, and so on) that identifies two opposite positions and the difference, if any, between them. A gap analysis may look like the following:

A typical discrepancy analysis might use the following set of questions.

1. Where are we now?

2. How important is this?

3. How well do you feel this is being done?

4. Where would we like to be?

5. What would it take to get us there?

By comparing the answers to each of the above questions, it is possible to ascertain where significant discrepancies might exist and what effort must be put forth for implementation.

Obtaining organizational needs from the employees is not an end in itself, but instead represents a valuable source of information regarding the current status of the corporate system. A needs assessment can provide the corporate system with some of the best available information on the immediate characteristics of the corporate training programs and those areas where attention and resources should be directed.

It is beyond the scope of this book to discuss the models of needs assessment; however, the reader may want to see Kaufman and English (1979) for more information on the subject. Instead, this section will present a simple needs assessment model based on four phases. They are

- *Phase 1: Set the needs assessment framework.* Here the corporate goals and objectives are set. The organization must know where it is going before it embarks on its journey.

- *Phase 2: Determine training discrepancies.* Essentially, this process involves a comparison of *what is* with *what should be* in three areas of the training setting. These areas are employment achievement, program and/or training operations, and preference assessment. The goal of this phase is to generate enough information so that a true and unbiased gap analysis may be performed. To do this, an objective reporting is essential.

- *Phase 3: Set tentative goal statements.* Management must analyze and interpret the data collected in phase 2 within the goal framework. Some of the alternatives are

  —Validate existing goal statements.

  —Develop new goals as indicated and supported by the discrepancy analysis.

  —Refine or revise existing goal statements.

  —Eliminate outdated goals.

- *Phase 4: Rank order the goals.* The final phase of the process involves determining the priority of goal statements and generating a plan for the actual implementation.

Essential to the effective conduct of the needs assessment is the sincere commitment of management at all levels. It is this commitment that will facilitate the process and bring it to its closure. The best one can hope—in any needs assessment—is to gather a reasonable amount of unbiased current input from the various employee groups. The instrument used for such a task is usually a survey instrument asking questions relative to the concern of the management team. The questions focus on what is and what should be. The actual development of the questions must be performed by a multidisciplined, cross-functional team of employees.

At this stage of the discussion, one may wonder why so much fuss is made over something that is—more or less—a common requirement. After all, some of the benefits of registration to the ISO standards were emphasized earlier, and it seems reasonable that no one in any organization should object to the implementation of such a standard. To be sure, in the automotive industry, the supplier base over the last decade has been initiated in both first- and second-party audits, and, as a consequence, suppliers are pretty much familiar with what is expected in the certification process. What is new and nontraditional is the method of receiving the certification—how the organization is expected to be third-party certified and to follow a strict rubric in the documentation process.

It should be reiterated that certification will indeed provide marketing opportunities for both existing and future customers. However, if this is the only reason for pursuing certification, the organization will shortchange itself of a greater opportunity to improve. The focus of the certification ought to be on establishing or improving the organization's quality system—something of which the automotive industry is very aware. To do that, one must know exactly where to start and how to go about it. As already stated, planning for the implementation will start with the needs assessment.

In a typical organization there are three areas where the four-phase model will interact with the organization. These are

1. *Organizational analysis*

   Determine the purpose and parameters of the needs analysis.

   Identify and gather information about opportunities for training in the organization.

Identify and gather information about the processes in the organization.

Gather all relevant information.

Analyze the information.

Determine the needs of the organization.

Report the findings.

2. *Work behavior analysis*

Identify the work to be examined as it relates to specific outcomes.

Construct a plan (flow) for the work behavior analysis. Job descriptions, job observations, interviews, and so on may be used.

Conduct an analysis of the plan or flow of the work behavior.

Gather all relevant information.

Determine the needs.

Report the findings.

3. *Individual capabilities analysis*

Identify the characteristics and/or capabilities of all employees for specific jobs.

Gather all relevant information.

Analyze and synthesize all data.

Determine the needs of individual employees.

Report the findings to decision makers.

Team Effort

To carry out an effective needs analysis, a team approach must be utilized. One of the reasons a team is important is that quality is a collective activity and it transcends both individuals and departments. In fact, for quality to really flourish, every employee and department in the organization must be committed to individual and collective responsibility. It is beyond the scope of this book to discuss the formation of teams, group dynamics, and empowerment; however, excellent discussions on these topics appear in Scholtes 1988, Jones and McBride 1990, Shonk 1992, Opper and Fersko-Weiss 1992, Aubrey and Felkins 1988, and Wellins, Byham, and Wilson 1991.

From an ISO and QS perspective, a team is also imperative. No one individual can complete the documentation or the implementation process alone. The tasks are lengthy, technical, specialized, and difficult. It is humanly impossible for one individual to have all the knowledge and experiences necessary to complete all the required tasks. One individual may be the leader (facilitator), but not the entire team.

From the very beginning, all work should be undertaken as a team project. A project managed by an appointed management representative is highly recommended. He or she will be responsible not only for overseeing the development and documenting stages, but also for maintenance of the implemented system. A typical candidate for such a task is the quality manager, with wide responsibility going outside his or her own department.

The project manager must define, to all team members, the requirements, the individual responsibilities, and the completion date. The project manager is responsible for accurate and timely data. As such, one of his or her responsibilities is to make sure that appropriate reviews are conducted, when applicable, with the team members.

ISO 9000 Implementation: A Project Management Approach

In order for quality to work, it must be a way of life for the entire organization. This means everyone in the organization has a stake in it. The chief executive, the engineer, the accountant, the janitor, and so on all have the responsibility and, hopefully, the authority to do a quality job.

The ISO 9000 standard series is one way to identify and document the system so that the essential elements of quality are covered. It is indeed the core minimum of all quality systems taking into consideration the entire organization. An overview of this relationship can be seen in Figure 6.1. Please note that in the figure ISO is not only the center of all functional departments in a given organization, but it also cuts through all the levels of personnel (both management and nonmanagement).

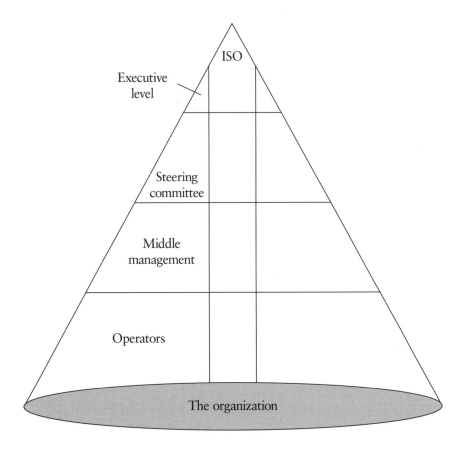

Figure 6.1. The relationship among the organization, its human resources, and ISO structure.

There are only a few basic principles associated with the ISO 9000 series, but incorporating them into the fundamental business activities may be the toughest task a management team performs. If these basic principles are allowed to develop, the very nature of the work may change. It is precisely this development of specificity that the QS-9000 series brings forward to amend the ISO requirements for the automotive industry.

To focus on this development, with the specific goal of improvement, at least five issues must be considered. All of them are based on a sound needs assessment.

1. *Establish important goals and objectives.* Management must answer Why ISO 9000 or QS-9000? Perhaps more importantly management must define what is reality from the current organization's point of view. Is management pursuing ISO 9000 or QS-9000 certification because of others or because of a general philosophy to be the best? In the automotive industry, this question can be a tricky one, as certification is a requirement of the industry as of September 1, 1994.

2. *Formulate actions via policies, programs, and procedures to achieve the desired goals.* Management must be fully committed to the program. The mode of operation should be to lead by example rather than to lead by memo or directive. It is imperative that policies, programs, procedures, and goals are based on being purpose led (vision), planning oriented, people centered, process focused, and performance based. Bias and partial information must be eliminated.

3. *Understand sources of resistance and neutralize them.* All work creates stress. All work contributes to resistance. Once new work is understood, however, it becomes the status quo. It is the job of management—either directly or indirectly—to make sure that everyone in the organization understands that conflict occurs—it is normal and expected. To minimize uncertainties and conflicts, use

effective vertical and horizontal communications. In addition, tactical and operational plans can be developed by empowered associates who know where the organization is going and are acutely familiar with the strengths and weaknesses of both the company and its competitors.

4. *Understand that change must not be forced, it must be managed.* All change is difficult. However, this difficulty can be minimized if the changes in an organization are well planned and managed. One method of implementing change is the pilot project, a temporary change management structure. Feedback to the pilot can help determine appropriate action to be taken on a more permanent basis.

5. *Understand that successful implementation requires education and training.* Everyone in the organization must have knowledge of the basics of ISO standards; not everyone in the organization needs to have formal experience or extensive knowledge. The distinction is important. Management must decide what kind(s) of education and training are appropriate for various employees based on such factors as employee function and level, organizational goals, and available facilities. Poor decisions cause waste of resources and, ultimately, delay in the implementation process.

How can management accomplish all these tasks? Project management (PM) should be at the core of the implementation strategy. (For greater discussion of project management than will be offered in this book, see Kerzner 1995, Frame 1994, Michael and Burton 1993, and Haynes 1989). A PM approach will facilitate the change at an optimum level throughout the organization. The kind of flexibility that is needed to ensure accurate information, proper direction, and project focus can only be accomplished through PM. The project manager is the appropriate, and perhaps the only properly qualified, professional to speed up the cumbersome communication paths of the hierarchical structure typical in most organizations. The project manager should be identified as the management representative

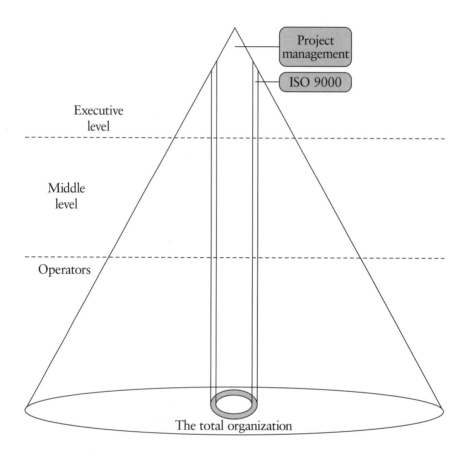

Figure 6.2. The relationship of project management, ISO 9000, and the organization.

as defined in ISO 9001 clause 4.1.2.3. The relationship of the organization, ISO, and PM can be seen in Figure 6.2.

How is PM going to help the implementation process? To answer that question, project management must be defined. By definition, project management focuses on the project (Kerzner 1995). A project is an undertaking that has a beginning and an end and that is carried out to meet established goals within

- Cost
- Schedule

- Quality objectives

- Optimum resource allocation

Project management brings together and optimizes (the focus is on the allocation of resources) rather than maximizes (concentrating on one thing at the expense of something else; maximization leads to suboptimization) resources, including skills, cooperative efforts of teams, facilities, tools, information, money, techniques, systems, and equipment.

Why PM as opposed to other management principles? There are at least two reasons. First, PM focuses on a project with a finite life span, whereas other organizational units expect perpetuity. Second, projects need resources on both a part-time and full-time basis, while permanent structures require resource utilization on a full-time basis. The sharing of resources may lead to conflict and requires skillful negotiation to see that projects get the necessary resources to meet objectives throughout the project life.

PM will ensure success of the implementation process by following the four phases of a project's life (Kerzner 1995). The four phases and the corresponding responsibilities of the project manager follow.

Phase	*Project manager responsibilities*
1. Define the project.	The primary concern of the project manager is to clarify the project and arrive at an agreement among all concerned about the scope, as well as the basic strategy for carrying it out. Specific activities may include
	• Studying, discussing, analyzing the focus of the project.
	• Writing the project definition.
	• Setting an end-result objective.

- Listing absolute and desired needs.

- Generating alternatives.

- Evaluating alternatives.

- Choosing a course of action.

2. Plan the project.   Planning means listing in detail what is required to successfully complete the project along the critical dimensions of quality, cost, and time. Specific activities may include

- Establishing, reviewing, modifying, the project objective.

- Choosing the strategy for achieving the objective.

- Breaking down the project into small steps.

- Determining the performance standards.

- Determining realistic time requirements.

- Determining the sequence of implementation.

- Designing a cost budget.

- Designing the staff organization (internal and/or external).

- Determining the appropriate training (internal and/or external).

- Developing policies and procedures.

3. Implement the plan.   The entire project is coordinated on an ongoing basis. Specific activities may include

- Controlling and/or monitoring the work.
- Negotiating changes.
- Providing appropriate feedback (formal or informal).
- Resolving differences.

4. Complete the project.   The goal of project management is to obtain client (in this case, management) acceptance of the project result. This means that management agrees that the quality specifications of the project parameters have been met. For this agreement to take place as smoothly as possible, an objective evaluation must take place based on measurable criteria defined in the early stages of the implementation. (The evaluation may or may not be the ultimate certification through a third-party registrar.) As part of the completion phase, it is imperative that follow-up steps are defined to make sure that the ISO system—now in place—will not fade away. The definition of this follow-up may be very specific, so that the continuation of the ISO system will be self-sustained.

Earlier, the implementation process was defined as a project. As long as that definition is used in the entire organization, PM is indeed one of the most appropriate ways to pursue implementation. A typical approach of PM may define the project initiation, the communication needs for the implementation process, the process itself, the ISO requirements, and the monitoring of the process. An example of the specific items under PM may follow the information in Figure 6.3.

Figure 6.3 defines a four-phase ISO 9000 implementation model with detailed applications in each phase. What is important, however, is that in this model the previous phases may or may not be completed. The implementation process can be parallel (for instance, between two different departments), horizontal (within a department), or vertical (involving the entire organization). The pace can be different for different departments and organizations.

Once PM is established and understood by employees, the organization is then ready for the full ISO 9000 implementation process. The implementation of ISO 9000 is indeed a process. It is not necessarily linear, but rather follows the four phases in Figure 6.4. Each phase defines a certain amount of content and understanding of the process. Based on a thorough needs assessment, this task of identification (content and understanding) becomes an easy and manageable one.

An overview of this implementation process is given in Figure 6.5. This figure not only identifies the four phases of PM, but also incorporates all the elements of the implementation process and their relationship to the actual certification process.

One of the most important steps in this figure is the registrar selection during phase 2. It may take some time to secure a registrar for the certification process. It has been reported that, as of this writing, some registrars have up to a 12-month waiting list. An organization desiring certification should take this possibility into account when planning.

In the next section, a more complete description of the model is given. Each stage is identified as a phase because in each phase

Phase 1	Management commitment	Establish an ISO 9000 implementation team of one person from each functional area.
		Train those selected in ISO 9000 requirements.
Phase 2	Structure setup	Capture company objectives in ISO 9000 format. Mission Goals Focus on continual improvement Policies and procedures Quality management commitment
Phase 3	Implementation	Make goal of ISO implementation and/or certification.
		Examine internal structure and compare it to ISO 9000. Determine the departmental objectives. Review structure of the organization. Review job descriptions. Review current processes. Review control mechanisms. Review training requirements. Review communication methods. Reports Meetings Record keeping Review all approval processes. Review risk considerations and how they are addressed. Review all outputs. Review all action plans.
Phase 4	Working with the registrar	Fulfill registrar requirements. Audit Surveillance Correction action Certification Recertification

Figure 6.3. ISO 9000 implementation model.

Phase 1*	Phase 2	Phase 3	Phase 4
Management commitment	*Structure setup*	*Implementation of procedures*	*Working with the registrar*
Initiate project	**Understand process**	**Give ISO 9000 training**	**Monitor progress**
Management planning and goal setting	Team flowcharting for process understanding and analysis	Executive training	Worker/operator control in process
Department business and technical commitment	Cause-and-effect analysis	Department training	Define quality manual, procedures, instructions, and forms as they relate to the specific department area
Quality team selected and active	Critical in-process parameters identified	Identify shortcomings in the system of quality (specific areas)	Internal audit
Training philosophy and tools of quality	Standard operating procedures review, equipment repair, preventive maintenance, and calibration	Define boundaries of responsibility	Visit by the registrar
Process definition and selection	Process input and measurement evaluation	Define limitations of resources	Official audit
Critical characteristics identified	Static process data collection	Review system for completeness	Follow-up and maintenance of certification

*This grid takes into consideration that the activities in previous phases may or may not be completed. The advantage of implementing ISO 9000 in any organization is that the implementation process can be parallel, horizontal, or vertical. The rate of implementation may indeed be different for each individual department. The long-term goal is to receive and keep the certification.

Figure 6.4. The ISO 9000 implementation process.

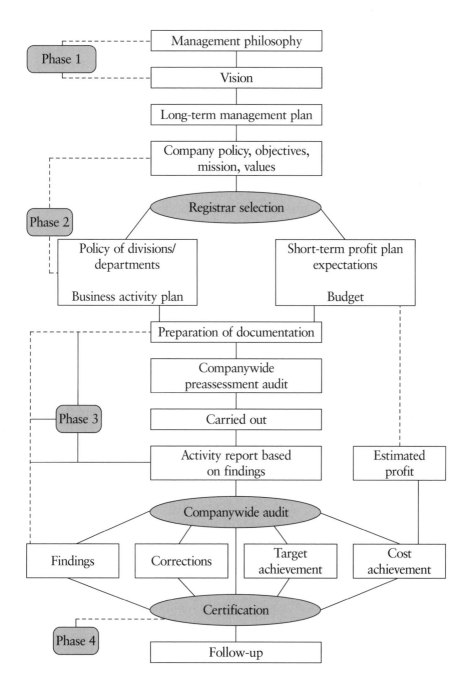

Figure 6.5. The PM structure of a companywide ISO 9000 implementation model.

there may be more than one item of concern. In fact, quite often there are a series of steps within each phase.

The Model of ISO 9000 Implementation

As has been discussed, the model of ISO implementation is based on the four phases of PM. The details for each phase follow.

Phase 1: Gain Management Commitment

Management must gain the commitment of the entire organization. In addition, an appropriate implementation strategy must be developed.

Phase 2: Set Up the Structure

Management must develop the organization and train the employees. This may be done through external or internal sources. The development of the organization deals with culture change and paradigm shifts. The training, on the other hand, is more extensive and requires a great commitment of time and all other resources.

To address the issue of ISO/QS-specific training, the best recommendation is generic training. Each organization is unique and has specific requirements of its own. However, a typical internal training curriculum for ISO 9000 includes the following.

Executive overview. A one-day training program should be designed as an introduction to ISO 9000 for executives and senior management. Its function is to educate; remove the mystery and misinformation from the subject; and help the executive team make informed decisions about the benefits, commitment, and plans required to obtain registration. General topics covered may include

- What is ISO 9000?
- What is QS-9000?

- Why are they needed?
- How are they organized?
- How do you receive certification?
- Is ISO 9000 certification equal to QS-9000? What are the differences? What are the similarities?

Twenty clauses of ISO 9001 and QS-9000. A one-day training program should be designed to address the 20 clauses of ISO 9001 and QS-9000 in detail. The focus should be on intent, meaning, and explanation. The audience for this training should be anyone in the organization who wants to learn more about ISO 9000 and QS-9000. General topics to cover include

- An overview of the entire ISO 9000 series
- The relationship of ISO 9000 series and QS-9000
- A detailed review of the contents of ISO 9001 and QS-9000
- An overview of the customer-specific contents of QS-9000
- Workshops applying the understanding of the requirements to simulated business situations
- A discussion on application of these standards to the organization in question

ISO 9000 and QS-9000 implementation. A two- to three-day training program on ISO 9000 and QS-9000 implementation should focus on a detailed action plan for successful implementation of a quality system. The target audience should be the middle managers, supervisors, and the personnel who will actually do the documentation. The length of the training depends on the background of the participants and their knowledge of documentation. General topics include

- ISO 9000 and QS-9000 overview
- A detailed explanation of ISO 9001

- A detailed orientation of QS-9000
- A general review of ISO 9004-1
- The implementation strategy for an organization
  - —Organize the effort
  - —Establish a management committee
  - —Document the system
  - —Provide for training
  - —Create a registration strategy
  - —Register the company

Documentation. Two days of training should be denoted to an in-depth review of ISO 9000 requirements and methods for documentation. This program should emphasize the different levels of documentation, how to keep it simple and effective, and how to maintain control of documentation. The audience for this training should be supervisors, operators, and anyone who is involved with documentation at any level or wants to understand the ISO documentation. General topics to cover are

- Overview of ISO 9000 series
- Overview of QS-9000 quality system requirements
- The importance of documentation
- Standard requirements
- Effective documentation
- Format and production issues of documentation
- Document control

Internal auditor. A two-day specialized training program should cover the concept of audit, setup and maintenance of an effective audit program, and the difference between inspection and audit.

The audience for this training should be a select group of employees who are going to be the designated internal auditors for the organization. General topics of discussion include

- General concepts of quality
- Quality system auditing practices for ISO 9000 and QS-9000
- Auditing to a standard
- The role of the auditor
- The audit
- The audit administration
- Ethics of audits
- Reporting the results
- Requirements for follow-up

Miscellaneous training. Depending on the needs of a specific organization the following additional training may be necessary.

- Needs assessment
- Project management
- Team building
- Lead auditor training
- Facilitator training
- Problem-solving techniques
- Flowcharting
- Statistical training
- Miscellaneous training (QFD, QOS, PPAP, APQP and control plan, VE, simulation, FTA, FEA, gauge R&R, and so on)

Consulting services. A given organization may require specific consulting services in any area. If additional services are required, a good rule of thumb is to do the training or provide the service on a just-in-time basis. Typical services are

- Specific training
- Readiness review
- Documentation assistance
- Specialized implementation services
- Supplier evaluation

The reader should be warned at this point. There are many consultants who claim they know how to "get" the certification for the organization. Of course, this is untrue. What a reputable consultant can do is help the organization through the maze. A consultant may coach and direct the process of implementation, but it is up to the members of the organization to be committed and do the work.

If your organization finds the need to hire a consultant, ask for at least the following documentation.

- Credentials
- Track record
- References
- Project plan

Phase 3: Implement Procedures and Document the Quality System

In phase 3 the structure of the documentation is defined and developed. Specifically, the following items are considered.

1. Identify all pertinent procedures, policies, and practices to meet specific ISO 9000 and QS-9000 requirements.

2. Prepare the documentation.

   a. The quality manual is a road map to the system, outlining the policies and objectives that relate to specific aspects of the system. The system, in this case, is the entire company.

   b. Procedures provide process descriptions and flowcharts of activities. They give more detail of what, who, where, and why an activity is carried out.

   c. Work instructions describe in step-by-step terms how to carry out a task. They are often called *standard operating procedures* (SOP), *standard job practices* (SJP), or *operating guides*. Work instructions must be revised and integrated into the overall documentation system.

   d. Forms are often used to collect information and record the completion of required quality activities.

   e. Sufficient records must be kept to provide objective evidence that the quality activities are being carried out.

For the relationship of the documentation between each of the tiers see Figure 4.1.

Phase 4: Work with the Registrar

Phase 4 provides for closure of the implementation process and is primarily controlled by the registrar. The company's contribution is minimal at this stage, although it is very important. Some of the characteristics of this phase are

- Preassessment
- Site visit (audit)
- Registration or corrective action
- Follow-up

Because the ISO 9000 structure provides for the foundation of quality, it is less stringent than both TQM and QS-9000 (see

Chapter 4). ISO 9000 provides for continual improvement in the scope of the standard, the corrective action subsection, and elsewhere. But, to move from ISO 9000 to TQM and QS-9000 requires an extension of all the basic quality guidelines as found in the ISO 9000 series and initiative in the principles of

- Measurement
- Customer satisfaction through active listening for customers' needs, wants, and expectations
- Continual adaptation to changing market conditions
- "The best is yet to come" attitude
- Market-driven attitude

A QS-9000 Implementation Model

There are many ways to implement a quality system, including a QS-9000 quality system. In this section we will address the implementation process generically but systematically. The approach is based on the following steps and is also shown pictorially in Figure 6.6.

Step 1. Management and union commitment. The requirements of QS-9000 should be explained and internalized. Furthermore, managers should form goals, costs, benefits, and a vision so that the information can be communicated to all employees.

Step 2. Select implementation team. Forming a team is very important. Employees with experience about the organization and who are respected by other employees should be members of the team. The members should be cross-functional, including both managers and labor leaders.

Step 3. Select a management representative. This individual will be expected to be the mediator between the team members, managers, and the affected employees. Therefore, this individual should have the respect of his or her employees and should be a good

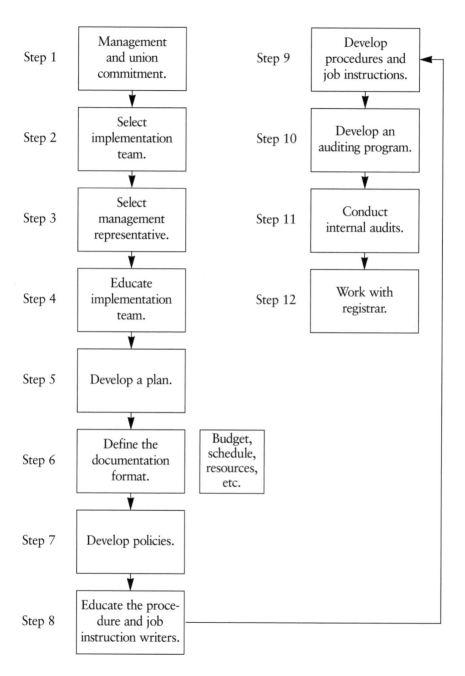

Figure 6.6. A QS-9000 implementation model.

communicator, have good leadership and organizational skills, and be willing to be a champion.

Step 4. Educate the implementation team. The team should be trained in the QS-9000 goals and requirements and, more importantly, on team dynamics and consensus building.

Step 5. Develop a plan. This is a crucial step primarily because, based on this plan, budgets, schedules, and other resources will be defined.

Step 6. Define the documentation format. This is perhaps one of the easiest steps in the QS-9000 implementation process. Typical activities of this step are to define the following:

- The tiers of the documentation (three as opposed to four)
- Numbering system
- Content headings or footers
- Approval blocks
- Content identified with prose, outline, flowchart, or combinations of these.

Step 7. Develop policies. Policies are generic statements that define the overview and intent of the quality system. (They are indeed the statements that make up the quality manual.) The team will identify and/or define the policies, but the managers and all the employees must review them to decide if they are appropriate and applicable to their function.

Step 8. Educate the procedure and job instruction writers. It is imperative that all employees responsible for writing procedures, job instructions, or both are appropriately trained. Knowledge and skills used in these activities are

- QS-9000 goals and requirements
- Flowcharting
- Knowledge about the tasks and/or processes
- Team dynamics and consensus building

Step 9. Develop procedures and job instructions. The concern here is to identify and document what you do. Specifically, the procedure will identify the who, what, and when, and the job instruction will describe how a job is done. Therefore, it is strongly suggested that the people who do the job be active participants. Sometimes cross-functional teams are used for the write-up. However, in all cases at the end, both the procedures and job instructions should be reviewed by the affected people, so they are familiar with them and follow them.

Step 10. Develop an auditing program. In this step the organization's management, the management representative, or a combination of both will select a pool of individuals to conduct internal audits and to ensure independence. Once the pool is selected, then appropriate training is conducted.

Step 11. Conduct internal audits. The idea of internal audits is to identify both shortcomings and exemplary items within the quality system and communicate them to management and appropriate personnel. If shortcomings are found, corrective action and follow-up are mandatory to improve the system. If exemplary items are found, then these items are also communicated so that they can be repeated in other areas.

Step 12. Work with the register. In this step, the registrar is contacted and the preassessment or assessment for the certification is planned.

Cost of Implementation

The discussion of implementation always raises the concern of cost for a program that requires such heavy documentation. Of course, implementation cost varies from company to company; but, some general guidelines will be given in this section.

The majority of the cost is an internal cost associated with writing manuals, procedures, instructions, and so on, rather than a cash disbursement to outsiders. The amount of these costs obviously depends on where your organization is in relationship to the requirements. In the automotive industry, for instance, the costs of implementing QS-9000 should be lower than average because the automotive industry has over the years disciplined itself to comprehensive documentation. What is needed now is the integration of that system into the new one.

In a July 1993 special report the *Continuous Improvement* newsletter published the survey results from a national study on ISO 9000 consultants (What does consultancy cost? 1993). Based on that study, there were 1800 consultants charging anywhere from $320.00 per day to $2000.00 per day, with an average fee of $958.36 per day.

A recent survey by Dusharme (1995) reports the following average costs.

Company size	Average cost	Average annual savings
Up to $50 million	$118,000	$57,000
$50–500 million	232,000	182,000
$500 million and up	445,000	410,000

Registered cost	Company size		
	Small	Medium	Large
Initial documentation review	$6,000	$10,000	$18,000
Follow-up (six months)	$2,500	$5,000	$7,000

From the author's experience (having participated in more than 30 implementations and registrations for both ISO 9001 and ISO 9002) the estimated costs are as follow.

Area	Low cost	High cost
Consulting (20–30 days)	$20,000	$50,000
Training (public seminars)	5,000	20,000
Software tools (QA applications, work processing)	–	20,000
Registrar		
Preassessment	5,000	10,000
Assessment	10,000	45,000
Annual surveillance	5,000	15,000
Subtotal	**45,000**	**160,000**
Internal costs (Meetings, writing manuals, reviews, visits) (approx. 10–24 months)	100,000	150,000
Total	**$145,000**	**$310,000**
Average	**$227,500**	

By now, ISO 9000 implementation costs are, for all intents and purposes, very steady and predictable. On the other hand, QS-9000 implementation costs are anything but steady and predictable. The only thing that can be said is that the costs for QS-9000 implementation should be much lower than those of the ISO 9000, since most, if not all, automotive suppliers have been involved with some kind of a quality system for some time.

In any case, Table 6.1 shows some costs with and without ISO 9000 certification as a base. The costs are based on Martin and Munro (1995) and a random survey from July–November 1995 conducted by Contemporary Consultants Co. (1995).

A Summary of ISO 9000 Implementation

The needs assessment will be the first step in the ISO 9000 implementation process. Once the needs assessment has been completed, a project management approach should be taken for the actual implementation phase.

Table 6.1. Costs associated with QS-9000 implementation, with and without ISO 9000 certification.

Area	With ISO base Low	High	Without ISO base Low	High
Consulting	$10,000	$15,000	$20,000	$ 45,000
Training	2,000	5,000	5,000	15,000
Computers (software, hardware	150	500	1,000	20,000
Registration:				
Preassessment	Free	5,000	4,000	10,000
Assessment	5,000	25,000	8,000	35,000
Annual surveillance	5,000	10,000	6,000	12,000
Subtotal	22,150	60,500	44,000	137,000
Average	**41,325**		**90,500**	
Internal costs:				
General education				
136 man-days @ $80/day	10,880			
160 man-days @ $80/day			12,800	
Documentation				
45 man-days @ $80/day	3,600			
60 man-days @ $80/day			4,800	
Management team and representative				
120 man-days @ $100/day	12,000		12,000	
Overall average	**67,805**		**120,100**	

The actual implementation process may be summarized with the following outline. Please note that the outline may be too prescriptive for your needs. Remember, this is only a guideline, and some of the items may not apply to some organizations. On the other hand, some organizations may require more.

A. Scope of the certification

—Location

—Business unit

—Product line

—Appropriate standard

B. Implementation team

—Project leader

—Core team

—Functional representatives

C. Education and training

—Public seminars

—Lead auditor training

—Orientation programs

—Documentation methods

—Internal auditor training

—Employee update meetings

—Networking

D. Effective use of consulting resources

—Primary benefits

—Suggestions

—Selection criteria

E. Documentation

—Generic structure

—Alternative structures

—Standard format

—Software tools

F. Operating the quality system

—Document control

—Internal auditing

—Corrective action

—Management review

G. Registrar selection

   —Services

   —Selection criteria

H. Third-party assessments

   —Preassessment

   —Initial assessment

   —Surveillance audits

A Summary of QS-9000 Implementation

A. Scope of the certification

   —Location

   —Business unit

   —Product line

   —Appropriate standard

B. Implementation team

   —Project leader

   —Core team

   —Functional representatives

C. Education and training

   —Public seminars

   —Lead auditor training

   —Orientation programs

   —Documentation methods

—Internal auditor training

—Employee update meetings

—Networking

D. Effective use of consulting resources

—Primary benefits

—Suggestions

—Selection criteria

E. Documentation

—Generic structure

—Alternative structures

—Standard format

—Software tools

F. Operating the quality system

—Document control

—Internal auditing

—Corrective action

—Management review

G. Specific selection of customer requirements.

H. Registrar selection

—Services

—Selection criteria

I. Third-party assessments

—Preassessment

—Initial assessment

—Surveillance audits

The reader should notice that the actual implementation process for QS-9000 is basically identical to the general ISO 9000 implementation. A major difference appears in QS-9000 section G, which defines specific customer requirements.

References

Aubrey, C. A., and P. K. Felkins. 1988. *Teamwork: Involving people in quality and productivity improvement.* White Plains, N.Y.: Quality Resources and Milwaukee, Wis.: ASQC Quality Press.

Contemporary Consultants Company. 1995. *Cost for implementing a QS-9000 system: A survey of automotive suppliers.* November. Southgate Mich.: Contemporary Consultants Co.

Dusharme, D. 1995. ISO 9000 certification costs. *Quality Digest* (January): 8.

Frame, J. D. 1994. *The new project management.* San Francisco, Calif.: Jossey-Bass Publishers.

Haynes, M. E. 1989. *Project management: Four steps to success.* Los Altos, Calif.: Crisp Publications.

Jones, L., and R. McBride. 1990. *An introduction to team-approach problem solving.* Milwaukee, Wis.: ASQC Quality Press.

Kaufman, R., and F. W. English. 1979. *Needs assessment.* Englewood Cliffs, N.J.: Educational Technology Publications.

Kerzner, H. 1995. *Project management: A systems approach to planning, scheduling and controlling.* 5th ed. New York: Van Nostrand Reinhold.

Martin, T. and R. A. Munro. 1995. Introduction to Automotive Quality. Auto-Tech 95 Introductory Tutorial. 19–21 September, Detroit, Michigan.

Michael, N., and C. Burton. 1993. *Basic project management.* Singapore: Singapore Institute of Management.

Opper, S., and H. Fersko-Weiss. 1992. *Technology for teams.* New York: Van Nostrand Reinhold.

Scholtes, P. R. 1988. *The team handbook.* Madison, Wis.: Joiner Associates.

Shonk, J. S. 1992. *Team-based organizations: Developing a successful team environment.* Homewood, Ill.: Business One Irwin.

Wellins, R. S., W. C. Byham, and J. M. Wilson. 1991. *Empowered teams.* San Francisco, Calif.: Jossey-Bass Publishers.

What does consultancy cost? 1993. *Continuous Improvement* (July): 4–5.

CHAPTER 7

ISO 9000 and Other Quality Systems

The ISO 9000 quality management system is only one of many systems used by different countries and industries to assess their quality. This chapter attempts to compare the ISO 9000 system with some of the most common systems used in the automotive industry. It is not intended to be an exhaustive discussion. Rather, it is hoped that the reader will be aware that (1) other quality systems do exist, and (2) the ISO 9000 structure is only a basic quality system that is, perhaps, the first step to world-class quality. QS-9000 will not be discussed in this chapter as it is based on ISO 9001, with additional requirements appropriate to the automotive industry.

As we have seen, the ISO standards were developed by a committee of quality professionals. These standards were in no way developed from scratch. In fact, they were developed by taking specific elements from other standards such as: military standards (MIL-I-45408, MIL-Q-9858A), nuclear power plant regulations (Appendix B to 10CFR50), British standards (BS 5750), medical device manufacturer regulations (the Food and Drug Administration's Good Manufacturing Practices), Canadian standards (Z299), and other regulations. The ISO standards are indeed what Arter (1992) called "a gourmet soup." Because the standard is a combination of other standards, it follows that there must be some common elements as well as some differences. Some of these will be reviewed.

Total Quality Management and ISO 9000

At no other time have two quality systems (movements) existed simultaneously. Both of them are very powerful systems. Their similarities are self-explanatory, while their differences are somewhat more convoluted. A brief description will be given for the latter. For a detailed discussion see Welch 1993, Harral and Berg 1993, and Finlay 1992.

Similarities. The similarities between ISO 9000 and TQM can be viewed as follows: quality philosophies, influence from other cultures, training and education, record keeping, customers, and subcontractor relationships.

Differences. The differences between ISO 9000 and TQM are more significant. They are views on success, views on the process, views on responsibility, and views on flexibility.

- *Views on success.* ISO 9000 uses registration as the measure of success. TQM, on the other hand, uses customer satisfaction as the measure of success.

- *Views on the process.* ISO 9000 emphasizes controlling processes and replicability. TQM, on the other hand, emphasizes process improvements as well as controlling good processes.

- *Views on responsibility.* In ISO 9000, the responsibility is assigned to anyone whose work affects the quality of the product. Quite often, management assigns a representative. In general, the ISO 9000 guidelines indicate that responsibility should be assigned to individuals. In contrast, TQM emphasizes teamwork and team involvement in implementing quality systems.

- *Views on flexibility.* ISO 9000 provides the quality system's structure, control, and adherence to procedures. As a consequence, it restricts the organization's freedom to change and adapt. These attributes are also against the TQM philosophy of removing barriers to rapid quality improvement.

Comparing ISO 9000 with Deming-Based TQM

ISO 9000 has clear requirements that may or may not be particularly significant in Deming-based TQM (DBTQM). ISO 9000 requirements dictate that contract review be addressed in very specific terms, while DBTQM leaves the details entirely up to the organization. Similarly treated are the issues of design control, inspection and testing, and much more.

In a very simplistic approach, one may argue that the basis of Deming-based TQM is statistical understanding, yet ISO 9000 treats statistical process control as something of an afterthought. Certainly DBTQM is much more than statistics and measurement, just as ISO 9000 is much more than a fast brush of quality in any organization.

ISO 9000 and the Malcolm Baldrige National Quality Award

Finlay (1992, 1) proposed that a comparison between ISO 9000 and the Malcolm Baldrige National Quality Award (MBNQA) may be an "apples-versus-citrus-salad comparison." He continues the analogy by saying that "ISO is like three starched white business shirts—small, medium, and large—form fitting, but not expected to cover the whole body." MBNQA, on the other hand, "is like a giant, one-size fits all T-shirt with 33 pockets in which specific articles are to be placed."

It is indeed difficult to compare the two systems. They are different in their purposes, assumptions, results, and evaluation. The MBNQA process is designed to recognize and award those firms with outstanding records of quality performance. While the use of ISO 9000 may be a good starting point in establishing a quality system, the criteria used in evaluating candidates for the MBNQA are much more detailed and extend beyond those areas covered by ISO 9000.

The MBNQA criteria are primarily results-oriented (though the organization is required to follow both results and process criteria), and cover all operations, processes, and work units of a company. The evaluation procedures emphasize the dynamics involved in the integration of all aspects of a firm's quality system and the firm's continuous improvements in quality (Breitenberg 1993). MBNQA requires specific organizational involvement and change.

The ISO 9000 requirements are clearly defined, but the organization has the freedom to define how these requirements will be met. ISO 9000 concentrates almost exclusively on results criteria, although process criteria may meet some ISO 9000 requirements, depending on the lead auditor.

ISO 9000 and Military Standards

While the specific differences between ISO 9000 and military standards are numerous, the general difference between the two is that of scope. All military standards are concerned with conforming supplies through the use of inspection programs. ISO 9000 is concerned with compliance and customer satisfaction (to a degree) through the use of quality management. The military standards system focuses on appraisal as the foundation of quality; whereas ISO 9000 attempts to address prevention and planning through management intervention as the foundation of the quality system.

References

Arter, D. R. 1992. Demystifying the ISO 9000/Q90 series standards. *Quality Progress* (November): 65–67.

Breitenberg, M. 1993. *ISO 9000: Questions and answers on quality, the ISO 9000 standard series, quality system registration, and related issues.* Publication number NISTIR 4721. Gaithersburg, Md.: National Institute of Standards and Technology, U.S. Department of Commerce.

Finlay, J. S. 1992. ISO 9000, Malcolm Baldrige award guidelines, and Deming/SPC-based TQM—A comparison. *Quality Systems Update* (August): 1–9.

Harral, W. M., and D. L. Berg. 1993. Implementing TQM in an ISO framework. *Automotive Division Newsletter* (fall): 9–11.

Welch, C. 1993. ISO 9000 and TQM: Finding balance. Paper presented at 1st Annual International Conference on ISO 9000, 1–2 November, Lake Buena Vista, Florida.

The Future of the ISO 9000 Series and QS-9000

Predicting the future of anything is risky at best. Predicting what the world holds in store for quality is even harder. Chapter 8, however, will present some general predictions based on the trends of the last couple years.

According to a survey by Mobil Company reported in the April 1994 issue of *On Q*, the total number of registrations to the ISO 9000 series standards grew by 70 percent during the first nine months of 1993 (Registration to ISO 9000 1994). Registrations grew to 45,000 in October 1993 from a 1992 year-end total of 26,400. As of this writing, the number is over 70,000. The same survey reported that the United Kingdom has been issued the greatest number of registrations, with a 62.5 percent share; the rest of Europe follows with a 21.5 percent share; Australia and New Zealand, 7.1 percent; North America, 4.7 percent; and the Far East, 3.5 percent. The survey further reported that the number of countries in which registrations were issued rose from 48 to 60— a 25 percent increase. The most dramatic increase in the number of registrations—over 150 percent—occurred in Japan and the United States. Singapore and Malaysia followed with about a 100 percent increase each, with Germany close behind.

A similar survey by Coleman (1994) reports that awareness of the ISO 9000 series standards rose from 69 percent in 1991 to 79 percent in 1994. The reasons for certifications have shifted as well. The chief reasons respondents cited for seeking certification are that it demonstrates a quality commitment to employees, it helps them compete in the international arena, and major customers simply demand it. Whereas in 1991 international growth was in the 90th percentile as the reason for certification, Coleman's study shows that 85 percent of the respondents claim that the driving force behind ISO certification was the customer.

The results of the surveys indicate that the ISO 9000 series is a world system—no longer pursued exclusively in the European Union. In fact, steps are being taken to create an international system for the recognition of ISO certificates. Toward that goal, the International Organization for Standardization and the International Electrotechnical Commission are being asked to set an ad hoc committee to develop the rules and guidelines for the system, define the responsibilities of its governing body, outline its operating method, and set a timetable for its establishment (U.S. proposes committee 1993).

Vision 2000

The International Organization for Standardization continues to develop industry-specific standards through Technical Committee (TC) 176 to avoid proliferation of individual standards throughout the world. The vision is to have a truly global marketplace by having an internationally accepted mechanism. This plan has been dubbed Vision 2000.

The goals of Vision 2000 may be categorized in the following areas.

1. Universal acceptance

   • The standards are widely adopted and used worldwide.

- Few complaints are received from users in proportion to the standards' use.

- Few sector-specific supplementary standards are being used or developed.

2. Current compatibility

   - Supplements to existing standards do not change or conflict with requirements in the parent standard.

   - The numbering and clause structure of a supplement remains the same as that of the parent document.

   - Supplements are not stand-alone documents. Rather, they are to be used with the parent document.

3. Forward compatibility

   - Revisions affecting requirements in existing standards are few in number and minor or narrow in scope.

   - Revisions are accepted for new and existing contracts.

4. Forward flexibility

   - Supplements are few in number, but can be combined as needed to meet the needs of virtually any industry, economic sector, or generic category of products.

   - Architecture of supplements allows new features or requirements to be consolidated into the parent document at a subsequent revision if the supplement's provisions are found to be used practically universally.

The essence, then, of Vision 2000 is to have standards that meet market needs. Central to this vision is the development of new standards that are responsive not only to the manufacturing industry, but to other sectors as well (for example, hardware, software, services, and processed materials). There is no value in a standard that, for whatever reason, is not wanted or used in the marketplace.

Publication of Vision 2000 documents is planned for late 1996. While the standards will not be specific to any industry or economic sector, additional product-specific documents continuing technical requirements for product test will be developed within industry/economic sectors.

Beyond the ISO 9000 Series

The ISO 9000 series standards answer many of the quality deficiencies and irregularities that many organizations are forced to suffer. It establishes the foundations of a consistent quality management system for any organization committed to quality. The standards allow for the expansion of that system through continuous improvement to reach a world-class level.

The ISO 9000 series, just like other quality systems, recognizes that quality is a journey, not the destination. As a consequence, continuous improvement defines a world-class, mature quality organization as one in which an integrated philosophy of improving productivity, quality, and quality of work life for all stakeholders is present. The intent for such organizations is to demonstrate consistent, measurable, and positive results (Scheffler 1993).

The ISO standards are so fundamental to overall quality that ISO/TC 176 is expanding its scope to specific industries through special directives and guidelines. The directives are intended to standardize the regulations across different countries, while the guidelines provide recommendations as to *how* to go about implementing the standard in a given organization.

There are many directives under consideration. Some of the most important pertain to the following topics (U.S. proposes committee 1993; Registration to ISO 9000 1994; Kolka 1994a, 1994b).

• *Machinery.* On January 1, 1995, safety requirements for many machine types, whether built in the EU or imported, became effective. The directive permits manufacturers to self-declare that their products conform to its requirements. Other machine types considered to have a higher risk of injury must follow a stricter certification procedure. The basic approach of the directive is safety integration. Safety is to be integrated at the design stage and maintained throughout the foreseeable lifetime of the machine.

• *Telecommunications.* The basic issues of this directive are conformity assessment, conformity requirements, and local representation.

• *Software.* The objectives of this directive are to ensure an adequate level of protection for those who create computer software and to promote the free circulation of computer software within the community. While the objectives seem to be straightforward, there are some concerns.

• Interpretation of ISO 9000-3 as a guide

• Scope of the software sector scheme

• Auditor qualification and certification process

• National accreditation process and recognition of accreditations

• Obtainability of customer input

• Information technology (IT) registration logo

• *Product safety.* This directive became effective June 29, 1994. It is aimed at the rapid exchange of information in the event of serious risk to the health and safety of consumers. The language of the directive is quite explicit concerning post-sales obligations. In defining a "safe" product, the directive identifies several points relevant to "high level of protection for the safety and health of persons, taking into account the following points in particular."

• The characteristics of the product including its composition, packaging, instructions for assembly, and maintenance

- The effect on other products where it is reasonably foreseeable that it will be used with other products

- The presentation of the product, the labeling, any instructions for its use and disposal, and any other indication or information provided by the producer

- The categories of consumers at serious risk when using the product, in particular, children

In addition, this directive requires that producers provide consumers with relevant information to help consumers assess product risks "throughout the normal or reasonably foreseeable period of its use" and

> *Adopt measures commensurate with the characteristics of the products which they supply, to enable them to be informed of risks which these products might present and to take appropriate action including, if necessary, with drawing the product in question from the market to avoid these risks (Kolka 1994b).*

- *Packaging.* The packaging and packaging waste directive covers all industrial, commercial, and household primary (sales), secondary (group), or tertiary (transport) packaging. Specifically, it defines packaging in all forms, prevention recovery, recycling, and disposal. Furthermore, it sets targets regarding the recovery of packaging waste at no later than five years, except for Greece, Ireland, and Portugal, which are allowed until December 31, 2005, with at least 25 percent recovery in the first five years.

A reader interested in more detailed information regarding the directives is encouraged to contact SIMCOM in Atlanta, Georgia, at 800-538-7673.

In addition to these areas, as of this writing, ISO TC 176 is working on the development of the following:

- Draft international standard (DIS) 8402-1, *Quality systems terminology* (imminent release expected)

- Draft international standard (DIS) 9004-3, *Quality management and quality system elements—Part 3: Guidelines for processed materials* (imminent release expected)

- Draft international standard (DIS) 9002-2, *Quality management and quality system standards—Part 2: Generic guidelines for the application of the certifiable standards—ISO 9001, 9002 and 9003* (imminent release expected)

- Draft international standard (DIS) 9004-4, *Quality management and quality system elements—Part 4: Guidelines for quality improvement* (imminent release expected)

- Committee draft (CD) 9004-6, *Quality management and quality system elements—Part 6: Guidelines quality plans*

- Working draft (WD) 9004-5, *Quality management and quality system elements—Part 5: Guide to quality assurance for project management*

- Working draft (WD) 10012-2, *Quality assurance requirements for measuring equipment—Part 2: Measuring assurance*

- Working draft (WD) 10014, *Guide to the economic effects of quality*

- Working draft (WD) 10015, *Continuing education and training guidelines*

One of the areas in which the International Organization for Standardization may have the most impact is the formation of ISO/ TC 207. The mission of TC 207 is to develop an international environmental management standard. Block (1994) suggests that this initiative reflects the recommendation of the Strategic Advisory

Group on Environment (SAGE), an ad hoc committee created by ISO in 1991 to explore the feasibility of creating an environmental management standard similar to the ISO 9000 series standards for quality management systems. The implications of such an environmental standard to the automotive industry may be profound, as, among other things, it would define the scope, direction, and specific requirements on a global basis. Furthermore it would define the reclamation of the product once its life has expired. As a prelude to such major changes, see BS 7750 (BSI 1992), Stamatis 1995, and ISO/DIS 14001 (1995).

Worldwide Acceptance

At the April 1993 Quality Expo International Conference in Chicago, Illinois, international speakers discussed how the ISO 9000 series standards are gaining acceptance around the world (Kochan 1993). That in itself is an excellent development; however, it is certainly not the end of the story.

Unless international harmonization and mutual recognition also are achieved, the ISO 9000 series will fail in its purpose of removing market barriers. Registrations, conformity assessments, and registration procedures must be recognized universally. This is far from reality as of this writing, but a number of national and international bodies are beginning to tackle the issue.

While in the short run there may be some difficulties of recognition, all key indicators show that the ISO standards are not a fad. They are the world standards of the future. Together with the directives and guidelines they offer to any organization the standardization and minimum consistency of a quality management system second to none. By having a common denominator of a quality system, organizations can make decisions on productivity, costs, and profitability based on sound comparisons. To be sure, individual industries may need to modify the standards to better fit their specific needs (for example, to address customer-specific requirements). However, the basic structure of the ISO 9000 series is indeed universal in its applicability.

The future is indeed bright for the ISO 9000 series standards. As time goes on, the difficulties, uncertainties, and points of conflict within the standards will be addressed. To expedite this resolution, the technical committees will strive to issue guidelines and directives for more uniformity.

The Future of QS-9000

It is really too early to assess the success of QS-9000. However, preliminary data from both the supplier base and the Big Three indicate that this is an excellent standardization method for quality. In addition, it has been rumored that RAB is very pleased with the contents and would like to implement the QS-9000 quality system in other industries as well. The acceptability of QS-9000 depends on the enforceability and auditing of the system by the Big Three. Furthermore, in terms of its adoption and use, the success of QS-9000 will be based upon the size and impact of the automotive industry in North America and subsequently, the U.S. automotive industry in particular.

The QS-9000 itself claims that the "document will supersede all editions" (Chrysler, Ford, and GM 1995, 2). Judging from the past records of the U.S. automakers, the odds are that QS-9000 will be a lasting success. The reason for QS-9000's success will be that it is a simple and methodical program that anyone interested in quality can follow without any major problems.

References

Chrysler Corporation, Ford Motor Company, and General Motors Corporation. 1995. *Quality system requirements: QS-9000.* Southfield, Mich.: Chrysler Corporation, Ford Motor Company, and General Motors Corporation.

Block, M. R. 1994. ISO/TC 207. *The European Marketing Guide* (March): 19–22.

British Standards Institution. (BSI). 1992. *BS 7750: Environmental management systems.* London: British Standards Institution.

Coleman, J. 1994. Qualifying a quality success. *Quality* (October): 4.

ISO/DIS 14001. 1995. Draft international standard 14001, *Environmental management systems—Specification with guidance for use.* Geneva, Switzerland: International Organization for Standardization.

Kochan, A. 1993. ISO 9000: Creating a global standardization process. *Quality* (October): 6.

Kolka, J. W. 1994a. EN 46000 and the EU medical devices. *The European Report on Industry* (March): 13–17.

———. 1994b. EU general product safety directive. *The European Marketing Guide* (June): 12.

Registration to ISO 9000 grows worldwide. 1994. *On Q* (April): 4.

Schleffler, S. 1993. What is world-class, mature quality? *Continuous Journey* (August/September): 12–13.

Stamatis, D. H. 1995. ISO 9000 and BS 7750. *Environmental Journal* (March): 15–21.

U.S. proposes committee on ISO 9000 and health care products. 1993. *ISO 9000 News* (July/August): 4.

Training Curriculum

In chapters 3, 4, and 6 training was identified as an indispensable characteristic in both the ISO 9000 series and QS-9000. In addition, it was implied that training is of major concern in the implementation process. Because of the importance of training, the curriculum for an appropriate ISO 9000 series or QS-9000 implementation will be outlined here. The curriculum is not a prescription for every organization. Rather, it provides the sequence for appropriate training. Each organization has to assess its own environment and then plan accordingly.

While this appendix attempts to give generic course outlines for the essential characteristics of any ISO 9000 implementation endeavor, the author recognizes that some organizations may need training in other areas as well. These areas may include project management, teams, employee empowerment, general quality training, specific quality tools (brainstorming, cause-and-effect diagramming, process flowcharting, FMEA, QFD, and so on).

Executive Training for ISO 9000 and QS-9000

The executive workshop is intended as an overview and a general review of the ISO 9000 series and QS-9000. Specifically, it may serve a variety of industries including automotive, electronics, plastics, steel, printing, paper, and many more. It may be followed by specific training in the areas of implementation strategies, writing the documentation, and auditing training.

I.   Overview
     A. The standards
     B. Product life-cycle wheel

II. Purpose of standards
     A. European Union
     B. Liability directives
     C. Safety directives
     D. Market demands

III. Historical perspective

IV. Future directions
     A. Vision 2000
     B. A single quality management system

V.   ISO 9000 acceptance
     A. European Union
     B. United States
     C. Worldwide

VI. ISO 9000 as a platform
     A. Overview of the clauses in ISO 9001
     B. QS-9000 platform
     C. Suppliers and their role

VII. ISO and other systems
     A. Quality management versus TQM
     B. Baldrige Award criteria versus ISO standards
     C. MIL-Q-9858A versus ISO standards
     D. General conclusions

VIII. Benefits
   A. Question of value
   B. Market and customer requirements

IX. ISO standards structure
   A. Overview of ISO standards structure
   B. Definitions
   C. Overview of the quality management system
   D. QS-9000 structure

X. Synopsis of the ISO 9000 series and QS-9000 requirements
   A. Implementation strategies
   B. Overview of documentation need and structure
      1. Define documentation needed for the organization
      2. Train your workforce in ISO 9000 and QS-9000
      3. Prepare for registration

ISO 9000 Series and QS-9000 Documentation Training

A two-day documentation training sessions provides the minimum requirements for an in-depth review of ISO 9000 series requirements and methods for documentation.

I. Overview of ISO 9000 series standards
   A. The International Organization for Standardization
   B. ISO 9000 series standards
   C. The need for standards
   D. Program administration
   E. Registration
   F. The connection between documentation and registration

II. The importance of documentation
   A. Drivers of the documentation process
   B. Benefits of proper documentation
   C. Appropriate and applicable documentation for ISO 9000 series standards

III. ISO 9000 series requirements
   A. Flexibility of requirements
   B. The ISO 9004-1 factor in the documentation process
   C. Formal versus informal documentation

IV. Format for documentation
   A. Structuring the documents
      1. Hierarchy
      2. Parsing
   B. Terminology
   C. Logical conventions and structure of writing
   D. Organization's conventions and structure of writing
   E. Cross-referencing

V. Contents of appropriate documentation
   A. Company mission and policy statements
   B. Quality system documentation
      1. Quality manual
      2. Procedures
      3. Instructions
      4. Forms
      5. Quality records
      6. Quality plans

VI. Writing the documentation
   A. Company mission and policy statements
   B. Quality system documentation
      1. Quality manual
      2. Procedures
      3. Instructions
      4. Forms
      5. Quality records
      6. Quality plans
   C. Quality standards and procedures development process

VII. Relationship of project life-cycle documents and design control

VIII. Document control
  A. Role of ISO 9004-1
  B. Variety of control method
  C. Approval authority
  D. Revision history
  E. Handwritten changes
  F. Obsolete documents

IX. Document production issues
  A. Effective documentation
    1. Keep it simple
    2. Know the audience
  B. Principles of good technical writing
    1. Form and format
    2. Structure
    3. Pagination
    4. Appearance
    5. Use of flowcharts, pictures, diagrams, figures, and tables
  C. Editing, reviews, and proofreading techniques
  D. Appropriate reading level

X. QS-9000 requirements

XI. Customer-specific requirements
  A. Chrysler
  B. Ford
  C. GM

ISO 9000 Series Standards and QS-9000 Audits

I. Structure of standards
  A. ISO 9000 series overview
    1. ISO 9000-1
    2. ISO 9001
    3. ISO 9004-1

    B. QS-9000 overview
       1. Relationship to ISO 9001
       2. Sector requirements
       3. Specific requirements
    C. Requirements for the audit
       1. General criteria
       2. QSA requirements

II. Audit planning
    A. Vision
    B. Goals and objectives
    C. Quality factors

III. Selection
    A. Establishing criteria
       1. Internal
       2. External
    B. Target suppliers
       1. Approved
       2. Preferred
       3. Certified

IV. Audits versus surveys
    A. Definition
    B. Purpose
    C. Location
    D. Timing
    E. Methods

V. Types
    A. Internal (first-party)
    B. External (second-party)
    C. Third-party

VI. Managing the audit
    A. Administration
    B. Documentation
    C. Registrars

VII. Planning the audit
    A. Procedures and policies
    B. Performance measurements

VIII. Mechanics
    A. Preparation (before the audit)
    B. Opening meeting
    C. Visit
    D. Review of findings (closing meeting)
    E. Follow-up
    F. Corrective action

General Information and Publications

Appendix B provides the reader with important information as to how to obtain standards, information, and funding for internal training.

Distributor of the QS-9000 Document

Automotive Industry Action Group (AIAG)
26200 Lahser Rd., Ste. 200
Southfield, MI 48034
Telephone: 810-358-3570
Fax: 810-799-4220

Distributor of the IASG Sanctioned QS-9000 Interpretations

ASQC
611 East Wisconsin Ave.
P.O. Box 3005
Milwaukee, WI 53201
Telephone: 800-248-1946 or 414-272-8575
Fax: 414-272-1734

Sources of General Standard Publications

National Technical Information Services (NTIS)
5285 Port Royal Rd.
Springfield, VA 22161
Telephone: 703-487-4650
Orders only: 800-553-6847
Fax: 703-321-8547

Superintendent of Documents
U.S. Government Printing Office (GPO)
Washington, DC 20402
Telephone: 202-783-3238
Fax: 202-512-2250

Global Professional Publications
15 Inverness Way E., P.O. Box 1154
Englewood, CO 80150-1154
Telephone: 800-854-7179
Local phone: 303-792-2181
Fax: 303-792-2192

Standards Code and Information (SCI) Program
National Institute of Standards and Technology (NIST)
Administration Bldg., Rm. A629
Gaithersburg, MD 20899

Please send a self-addressed mailing label when requesting publication information from SCI.

The National Center for Standards and Certification Information (NCSCI)
National Institute of Standards and Technology
TRF Bldg., Rm. A163
Gaithersburg, MD 20899
Telephone: 301-975-4040

For assistance in obtaining information on current U.S. and foreign standards, regulations, and certification information.

Sources of Standards

Note—Copies of standards can be obtained from the respective issuing organization and/or these sources.

American National Standards Institute (ANSI)
11 W. 42nd St., 13th Floor
New York, NY 10036
Telephone: 212-642-4900
Fax: 212-398-0023
Orders only: 212-302-1286
Telex: 42 42 96 ANSI UI

ANSI-approved industry standards, international and foreign standards, select draft CEN/CENELEC standards, draft ISO standards

Global Professional Publications
15 Inverness Way E., P.O. Box 1154
Englewood, CO 80150-1154
Telephone: 800-854-7179
Local phone: 303-792-2181
Fax: 303-792-2192

Industry standards, federal standards and specifications, military standards and specifications, international and foreign standards

National Standards Association (NSA)
1200 Quince Orchard Blvd.
Gaithersburg, MD 20878
Telephone: 800-638-8094
Local phone: 301-590-2300
Fax: 301-990-8378
Telex: 44 6194 NATSTA GAIT

Industry standards; federal and military standards, specifications, and related documents; NATO standards, aerospace standards

General Services Administration (GSA)
Federal Supply Service Bureau
Specifications Branch
490 E. L'Enfant Plaza, S.W.
Ste. 8100
Washington, DC 20407
Telephone: 202-755-0325 or 0326
Fax: 202-205-3720

Federal standards and specifications

Naval Publications and Forms Center
Attn: NPODS
5801 Tabor Ave.
Philadelphia, PA 19120-5099
Inquiries only: 215-697-2667
Fax: 215-697-5914

Department of Defense (DOD)-adopted documents, naval publications, military manuals, and other related forms

Standardization Document Order Desk
Naval Publications Printing Service
700 Robbins Ave., Bldg. 4, Section D
Philadelphia, PA 19111-5094
Telephone: 215-697-2179
Fax: 215-697-2978

Military standards, specifications, and handbooks; federal standards and specifications

Document Center
1504 Industrial Way, Unit 9
Belmont, CA 94002
Telephone: 415-591-7600
Fax: 415-591-7617

Industry standards, federal standards and specifications, military standards and specifications, international and foreign standards

Information Handling Services (IHS)
P.O. Box 1154
Iverness Way E.
Englewood, CO 80150
Telephone: 800-241-7824
Local phone: 303-790-0600
Fax: 303-799-4097
Telex: 4322083 IHS UI

For IHS subscribers only—International and foreign standards, industry standards, federal standards and specifications, military standards and specifications, select European standards (CEN/CENELEC)

Standards Sales Group (SSG)
9420 Reseda Blvd., Ste. 800
Northridge, CA 91324
Information and quotes: 818-368-2786
Orders only: 800-755-2780
Fax: 818-360-3804

International and foreign standards, publications, and other reference materials; translations service; U.S./foreign general regulatory compliance information

Sources for Additional Information on NIST-Related Activities and Organizations/Documents

NIST's National Voluntary Laboratory Accreditation Program (NVLAP)

NVLAP/NIST
Bldg. 411, Rm. A162
Gaithersburg, MD 20899
Telephone: 301-975-4042
Fax: 301-926-2884

The Malcolm Baldrige National Quality Award Program

Office of Quality Programs/NIST
Bldg. 101, Rm. A537
Gaithersburg, MD 20899
Telephone: 301-975-3771

NIST's Calibration Program

Calibration Program/NIST
Bldg. 411, Rm. A104
Gaithersburg, MD 20899-0001
Telephone: 301-975-2002
Fax: 301-926-2884

NIST's Standard Reference Materials Program

Standard Reference Materials Program/NIST
Bldg. 202, Rm. 204
Gaithersburg, MD 20899-0001
Telephone: 301-975-6776
Fax: 301-948-3730

NIST's Standard Reference Data Program

Standard Reference Data Program/NIST
Bldg. 221, Rm. A320
Gaithersburg, MD 20899-0001
Telephone: 301-975-2208
Fax: 301-926-0416

ASQC standards, publications, activities, and services; ISO/TC 176's activities

ASQC
611 E. Wisconsin Ave., P.O. Box 3005
Milwaukee, WI 53202
Telephone: 800-248-1946 or 414-272-8575
Fax: 414-765-8661

The Registrar Accreditation Board's (RAB) program

Registrar Accreditation Board
611 E. Wisconsin Ave., P.O. Box 3005
Milwaukee, WI 53202
Telephone: 800-248-1946 or 414-272-8575
Fax: 414-765-8661

ANSI's activities or to purchase copies of ISO draft/final standards, other documents, magazines, newsletters, or copies of European standards (ENs)

The American National Standards Institute
11 W. 42nd St., 13th Floor
New York, NY 10036
Telephone: 212-642-4900
Fax: 212-302-1286

Irwin's registered company directory, Quality Systems Update *newsletter, and other publications*

Irwin Professional Publishing
133 Burr Ridge Pkwy.
Burr Ridge, IL 60521
Telephone: 708-789-5178
Fax: 708-789-6940

The Aerospace Industries Association's (AIA) activities

Aerospace Industries Association
1250 Eye St., N.W.
Washington, DC 20005
Telephone: 202-371-8400

The Netherlands' RvA program

Raad voor de Certificatie
Stationseg 13F, 3972 KA Driebergn
Telephone: +31 34 351 2604
Fax: +31 34 351 8554

The British Institute of Quality Assurance's (IQA) quality system assessor registration program

The Secretary to the Board
National Registration Scheme for Assessors of Quality Systems
The Institute of Quality Assurance
10 Grosvenor Gardens, London, U.K. SWIW ODQ
Telephone: 44-171-730-7154

The Standards Council of Canada (SCC) Program

Standards Council of Canada
45 O'Connor St., Ste. 1200
Ottawa, Ontario K1P 6N7 Canada
Telephone: 613-238-3222
Fax: 613-995-4564
The European Organization for Testing and Certification

EOTC
Rue Stassart 33, 2nd Floor
B-1050 Brussels, Belgium
Telephone: +32 2 519 6969
Fax: +32 2 519 69 17/19

The International Electrotechnical Commission's (IEC) Quality Assessment System for Electronic Components (the IECO system)

Electronic Components Certification Board (ECCB)
Electronic Industries Association (EIA)
2001 Pennsylvania Ave., N.W.
Washington, DC 20006
Telephone: 202-457-4967

Trade Adjustment Assistance Centers

Perhaps the most useful government program to manufacturers is the Trade Adjustment Assistance Center (TAAC). In this section an overview is given and some of its functions are discussed. In addition, the TAAC locations are identified.

Trade Adjustment Assistance (TAA) is a program sponsored by the U.S. Department of Commerce to give financial help to U.S. manufacturers that have been hurt by direct import competition. Examples of industries that may apply for assistance are diverse.

Aircraft components	Housewares
Automotive components	Leather and vinyl products
Computer controls	Material handling equipment
Electrical components	Printing equipment
Forgings	Tools, dies, patterns, and molds
Apparel	Industrial fasteners
Boat accessories	Machine tool accessories
Die castings	Plastics
Fans	Screw machine products
Furniture	Video equipment
Agricultural implements	Industrial knives
Compressors	Machine tools
Electric motors	Metal stamping and assembly
Ferous and nonferous	Power transmission components
foundries	Wood products/fencings
Glass	

In order to obtain benefits, a company must show that it has lost sales and/or production because of increased imports of competitive products, and that its workforce has been, or is likely to be, reduced. A small amount of paperwork is necessary, giving a brief description of the company and its products along with some data on sales and employment. Usually, the staff of the regional center will coordinate the preparation of the necessary information at no cost to the company.

Once the company is accepted into the program, a business-building strategy is developed tailored to the company's needs. Initially, the company's management meets with the center's representative to prepare an analysis of the company's manufacturing operations, marketing programs, and financial condition. The experts at TAAC will identify the company's strengths as well as weaknesses and present recommendations to the company's management to capitalize on those strengths and eliminate or minimize any weaknesses.

When this phase has management's approval, the TAAC team, working with the organization's management, will then prepare a business plan that describes the actions the company will take to implement its strategy. Developing the business plan is a cost-shared activity in which the Department of Commerce will pay three-fourths of the costs. The business plan is then submitted to the Department of Commerce for review and acceptance (which usually takes only 10 days). Once the plan is approved, the special consulting expertise the company needs can be provided. Requests for proposals are sent to a list of qualified consultants developed by your company and TAAC. The cost of these consulting services is shared between the company and the Department of Commerce, in accordance with the business plan previously approved.

What is remarkable about the services that TAAC provides is that, once a company has been established as eligible, implementation of the company's plan can begin in 16–20 weeks.

Examples of technical assistance available through the program include

- *Marketing*
  Analysis of competition
  Sales strategy
  Production line evaluation
  Sales forecasting
  Customer service audits
  Advertising and sales promotion review
  Market planning
  Distributor search and selection
  Pricing/quoting
  Sales organization restructure
  Market research
  Export development

- *Manufacturing/industrial and systems engineering*
  Product improvement
  Facility equipment layout
  Material handling methods
  Manufacturing technology audit
  Inventory control reduction
  Production scheduling control
  Process planning and control
  Quality assurance programs
  Statistical process control
  CAD/CAM
  Employee training
  Product testing
  Engineering specifications
  Product design and enhancement
  Equipment utilization surveys
  TQM/ISO training

- *Financial and general management*
  Profit planning
  Organizational analysis
  Financial reporting systems
  Electronic data processing enhancements/custom programming
  Electronic data processing conversion projects
  Cost accounting systems
  Expansion, diversification, and divestiture studies
  Budgeting
  Variable cost analysis
  Computer systems evaluation
  Manufacturing resource planning
  Material requirements planning
  Cash flow analysis
  Human resources planning/executive search

The specific TAA process is as follows. There are four phases that a company must go through before the TAA program will help.

1. *Eligibility.* In order to be certified eligible for TAA a firm must demonstrate each of the following:

—That a significant number or proportion of workers have been laid off or had their hours reduced, or there is a threat that workers may have to be laid off or have their hours reduced.

—That sales (in either units or dollars) or production or both have declined in absolute terms in the recent 12-month period compared with the preceding 12-month period, or there is a long-term declining trend. Alternatively, a firm can show a decline in one or more product lines, if they make up at least 25 percent of the company's total sales.

—That increases of imports of articles similar to or directly competitive with products produced by the firm contributed importantly to these problems.

In addition, the Department of Commerce must be able to determine that there has been an increase in imports, in either absolute amount or relative to domestic production, of like or directly competitive products into the United States in the past year.

2. *Application for certification of eligibility.* During this second stage the representatives of the TAA help the firm complete a petition for eligibility. Approximately 85 percent of the work is done by the center's staff, free of charge. The completed petition is sent to the U.S. Department of Commerce.

The U.S. Department of Commerce Office of Trade Adjustment Assistance (OTAA) has five calendar days to accept the petition for further investigation. After accepting the petition, OTAA has 60 business days to decide if the firm is eligible for assistance.

At this point, a center project manager is assigned to the firm to become familiar with the company's situation.

3. *Diagnostic survey/adjustment plan.* After the firm is certified and a cost-share agreement is signed, the center project manager will work with the firm to perform a diagnostic analysis of its operations that indicates areas of strength as well as areas that can be improved. The diagnostic then becomes the basis for developing a strategic adjustment plan to combat the adverse effects of import competition. The TAA program pays 75 percent of the cost of developing the adjustment plan, which often incorporates ideas currently being considered by the firm's senior officers. The strategic plan focuses on several critical activities that will prove most beneficial. Such a plan might call for implementation of advanced production technology, new marketing and sales strategies, new product lines, and/or process or office automation.

4. *Implementation.* After the adjustment plan is approved, competitive bids in accordance with government bidding guidelines are obtained from appropriate consultants or service firms. Once a firm or a consultant has been chosen, contracts are signed stipulating responsibility for cost of implementation. The TAA program will pay for up to 50 percent of the implementation of the plan exclusive of product prototypes, advertising, or equipment. In cases where outside consultants are involved, TAAC is required to monitor progress.

As mentioned previously, free assistance is available for the preparation of an application. However, the company is responsible for the following costs.

- 25 percent of the cost of assistance in preparing a diagnostic survey and business plan

- 50 percent of the cost of assistance to implement the business plan. Technical assistance can include outside professional assistance (for example, a consultant). It cannot include ordinary purchased services (for example, advertising) or capital equipment, or pay for in-house personnel. The adjustment proposal must also demonstrate that the firm will make all reasonable efforts to use its own resources to implement the plan.

The program's share of the total cost of implementation assistance is limited to the following:

50 percent of the first $95,000 of total cost

45 percent of the cost from $95,001 to $105,000

35 percent of the cost from $105,001 to $115,000

25 percent of the amounts in excess of $115,000

TAAC Locations

New England TAAC
Richard McLaughlin, Director
New England TAAC
120 Boylston St.
Boston, MA 02116
Telephone: 617-542-2395
Fax: 617-542-8457

Connecticut, Rhode Island, Vermont, New Hampshire, Massachusetts, Maine

New Jersey TAAC
John Walsh, Acting Director
NJ Economic Development Authority
Capital Place One-CN 990
200 S. Warren St.
Trenton, NJ 08625
Telephone: 609-292-0360
Fax: 609-292-0368

New Jersey

New York TAAC
John Lacey, Director
New York TAAC
117 Hawley St., Ste. 102
Binghampton, NJ 13901
Telephone: 607-771-0875
Fax: 607-724-2404

New York

Mid-Atlantic TAAC
William Gates, Director
Mid-Atlantic TAAC
486 Norristown Rd., Ste. 130
Blue Bell, PA 19422
Telephone: 215-825-7819
Fax: 215-825-7834

Pennsylvania, Delaware, Maryland, Virginia, West Virginia,
District of Columbia

Midwest TAAC
Howard Yefsky, Director
Applied Strategies Int'l.
150 N. Wacker Dr., Ste. 2240
Chicago, IL 60606
Telephone: 312-368-4600
Fax: 312-368-9043

Illinois, Minnesota, Iowa, Wisconsin

Northwest TAAC
Ronald Horst, Director
Bank of California Center
900 4th Ave., Ste. 2430
Seattle, WA 98164
Telephone: 206-622-2730
Tax: 206-622-1105

Alaska, Idaho, Montana, Oregon, Washington

Southeastern TAAC
Charles Estes, Acting Director
GA Institute of Technology Research Institute
151 6th St.
O'Keefe Bldg., Rm. 224
Atlanta, GA 30332
Telephone: 404-894-3858, 6789, 6106
Fax: 404-853-9172

Alabama, Tennessee, Kentucky, Mississippi, Georgia,
North Carolina, South Carolina, Florida

Southwest TAAC
Robert Velasquez, Director
Southwest TAAC
301 South Frio St., Ste. 225
San Antonio, TX 78207
Telephone: 210-220-1240
Fax: 210-220-1241

Texas, Louisiana, Oklahoma

Mid-America TAAC
Paul Schmid, Director
Univ. of Missouri at Columbia
University Place, Ste. 1700
Columbia, MO 65211
Telephone: 314-882-6162
Fax: 314-882-6156

Missouri, Kansas, Arkansas

Great Lakes TAAC
Maureen Burns, Director
University of Michigan School of Business Administration
506 E. Liberty St.
Ann Arbor, MI 48104-2210
Telephone: 313-998-6213
Fax: 313-998-6224

Michigan, Ohio, Indiana

Rocky Mountain TAAC
Robert Stansbury, Director
Rocky Mountain TAAC
5353 Manhattan Cir., Ste. 200
Boulder, CO 80303
Telephone: 303-499-8222
Fax: 303-499-8298

Colorado, Utah, Nebraska, South Dakota, Wyoming,
New Mexico

Western TAAC
Daniel Jimenez, Director
USC-WTAAC
3716 S. Hope St., Ste. 200
Los Angeles, CA 90007
Telephone: 213-743-8427
Fax: 213-746-9043

Arizona, California, Nevada, Hawaii

Production Part Approval Process Overview

In this appendix the intent is to summarize the production part approval process (PPAP). For the detailed content of this methodology, see the Chrysler, Ford, and GM manual by the same title (distributed by AIAG).

Overview

The PPAP is basically a system by which the supplier makes sure that all customer engineering design records and specification requirements are properly understood and that the process has the potential to produce a product meeting these requirements during an actual production run. As a consequence to this requirement, the Task Force has developed a generic methodology for approval, as well as some standardized forms. Following are the steps of the standardized process.

1. *When approval is required.* The manual identifies 11 specific situations in which approval is necessary, including new items, corrections, and/or modification of items.

2. *Requirements for approval.* The manual identifies 14 items that are required by this process, including failure mode

and effects analysis, process flowcharts, process performance evaluation, control plans, and design records.

3. *Submission levels.* The manual identifies five different levels of sample submission, with each level separately defined. It is the customer's choice to define the submission level.

4. *Process requirements.* The manual identifies 10 major categories under this requirement. They are as follows:

   • Drawings and sketches

   • Specific inspection or test device

   • Customer-identified special characteristics

   • Preliminary process performance evaluation

   • Appearance approval requirements

   • Dimension evaluation

   • Material tests

   • Performance tests

   • Part submission warrant

   • Engineering changes

   • Multiple cavity molds, tools, dies, and patterns

5. *Records and master sample retention.* In this section the manual defines the need for both records and retention periods.

6. *Part submission status.* In this section the manual defines the disposition of the submission in three categories.

   • Production approval

   • Interim approval

   • Rejected

7. *Appendix A.* The standard forms for submission, appearance approval report, and production part approval material test results are displayed.

8. *Appendix B. Chrysler-specific instructions.* There are seven specific instructions.

   • Submission levels

   • Interim approval

   • Laboratory approval

   • Checking aids

   • Clarification of customer

   • Appearance approval requirements

   • Supplier request for product change

9. *Appendix C. Ford-specific requirements.* There are nine requirements.

   • Item approval

   • Material approval

   • Interim approval

   • Control plans

   • Supplier request for engineering approval

   • Engineering specifications

   • Substance use restrictions

   • Significant products runs

   • Appearance item approvals

10. *Appendix D. General Motors instructions.* There are 10 requirements, given as guidelines and explanations. They are all self-explanatory.

11. *Appendix E.* This appendix provides a cursory change summary from the previous edition.

12. *Glossary.* This glossary identifies terms and their definitions as used in the PPAP.

Advanced Product Quality Planning Overview

This appendix summarizes the advanced product quality planning (APQP) process. For the detailed content of this methodology, see the Chrysler, Ford, and GM manual by the same title (distributed by AIAG).

APQP is a structured method of defining and establishing the steps necessary to ensure that a product satisfies the customer. The goal is to facilitate communication with everyone involved to ensure that all required steps are completed on time. It is a team endeavor and is dependent upon a company's top management commitment in achieving customer satisfaction.

As defined by the Task Force, the APQP is a six-step approach.

1. *Plan and define the program.* There are at least 13 areas of concern in this step. Some of the most critical are

   - Voice of the customer

   - Business plan

   - Benchmark data

   - Process assumptions

   - Customer inputs

- Goals
- Preliminary information regarding bill of material, process flowchart, and special characteristics
- Management support

2. *Product design and development.* There are at least 13 areas of concern in this step. Some of the most critical are

- FMEA
- DMA
- Material specifications
- Gauges and testing equipment requirements
- Feasibility commitment and management support

3. *Process design and development.* There are at least 12 areas of concern in this step. Some of the most critical are

- Packaging standards
- Process flowchart
- Floor plan layout
- Characteristics matrix
- FMEA
- Process instructions
- Preliminary process capability study

4. *Product and process validation.* There are at least eight areas of concern in this step. Some of the most critical are

- Production trial run
- Production part approval
- Packaging evaluation
- Production control plan

5. *Feedback, assessment, and correction action.* There are at least three areas of concern. They are

- Reduced variation
- Customer satisfaction
- Delivery and service

6. *Control plan methodology.* There are at least three areas of concern. They are

- Control plan column descriptions
- Process analysis
- Supplements, as needed

Select Bibliography

Ali, N. S. 1994. Developing 20/20 foresight. *CFO* (April): 48–53.

Block, M. R. 1994. ISO/TC 207: Developing an international environmental management standard. *European Marketing Guide* (March): 12–14.

Bobbit, C. E., Jr. 1993. Conduct more effective audits. *Quality Progress* (October): 60–63.

Byrnes, D. J. 1993. ISO 9000-style eco-audits. *PI Quality* (November/December): 3.

Chauvel, A.-M. 1994. Quality in Europe: Toward the year 2000. *Quality Management Journal* (January): 71–77.

Control software: Function point analysis and controls software. 1994. *ESD Technology* (March): 28–30.

Cook, N. P. 1993. Quality system, poor products? *ISO 9000 News* (July/August): 2.

Durant, A. C., and I. Durant. 1993. The role of ISO 9000 standards in continuous improvement. *Quality Systems Update* (October): 19–24.

Durant, I., C. McRobert, D. Middleton, and J. Tirato. 1992. Document and data control requirements of the ISO 9000 series standard. *Quality Systems Update* (May): 32–34.

Dzus, G. 1991. Planning a successful ISO 9000 assessment. *Quality Progress* (November): 25–28.

Dzus, G., and E. G. Sykes Sr. 1993. How to survive ISO 9000 surveillance. *Quality Progress* (October): 58–62.

Eade, T., and D. J. Byrnes. 1993. Documentation per ISO 9000. *PI Quality* (September/October): 2–3.

Earnshaw, D. 1993. The EC's eco-management and audit scheme. *EC Marketing Guide* (November): 16–17.

Edelstein, D. V. 1993. Software. *EC Report on Industry* (November): 11–13.

Egan, L. 1993. Software configuration management. *Continuous Improvement* (November): 1–4.

Environmental leadership. 1993. *Leaders* (July/August/September): 58–62.

The environmental standard—BS 7750. Parts 1 and 2. 1993. *Continuous Improvement* (August): 1–4; (September): 1–3.

Finlay, J. S. 1992. ISO 9000, Malcolm Baldrige award guidelines and Deming/SPC-based TQM—A comparison. *Quality Systems Update* (August): 1–9.

Garavaglia, P. L. 1993. How to insure transfer of training. *Training and Development* (October): 65–68.

Gladis, S. D. 1993. Are you the write type? *Training and Development* (July): 46–48.

Goult, R. 1992. ISO implementing an ISO 9000 series. *Quality Systems Update* (January–May): 12–14.

Grounds, R. 1993. Employee involvement: A major change in direction. *Quality Digest* (October): 30–32.

Guzzetta, S. 1993. How ISO 9000 changed supplier quality assurance. *PI Quality* (September/October): 3.

Hayes, R. H., and S. C. Wheelwright. 1984. *Restoring our competitive edge: Competing through manufacturing.* New York: John Wiley & Sons.

Health care TC forming. 1993. *ISO 9000 Journal* J-3 (November): 5.

Hovermale, R. A. 1994. ISO 9000—Continual improvement. *European Marketing Guide* (February): 23–25.

Howe, K. R., and K. C. Dougherty. 1993. Ethics, institutional review boards, and the changing face of educational research. *Educational Researcher* (December): 12–15.

How to implement ISO 9000. 1993. *Continuous Improvement* (April): 1–4.

How to prepare for ISO 9000. 1993. *Continuous Improvement* (October): 1–3.

ISO 9000 and inspection. 1993. *Continuous Improvement* (July): 2–3.

Jeffrey, N. 1994. Waste not . . . Minimizing and disposing of hazardous waste requires more than lip service. *American Printer* (January): 56–61.

Kinni, T. B. 1993. Preparing for fast-track ISO 9000 registration. *Quality Digest* (October): 16–19.

———. 1994. Reengineering primer. *Quality Digest* (January): 26–31.

Kochan, A. 1993. ISO 9000: Creating a global standardization process. *Quality* (October): 4.

Kolka, J. D. 1993. ISO 9000 and EC medical devices. *EC Report on Industry* (November): 14–15.

———. 1994. Product design, product software and product liability. *European Marketing Guide* (March): 25–27.

Kromrey, J. D. 1993. Ethics and data analysis. *Educational Researcher* (May): 3–5.

Landrum, R. 1993. 12 reasons to implement ISO 9000. *Quality Digest* (December): 12–16.

LeDoux, T. J. 1993–94. ISO 9000: What you don't know might hurt you! *Continuous Journey* (December/January): 6–8.

Mar, W. 1993. Seven keys to better project teams. *Quality Digest* (October): 21–23.

Marash, I. R. 1994. ISO 9000 and the medical device GMP. *European Report on Industry* (February): 7–9.

McIntosh, B. 1993. European Community legislation on machinery. *EC Report on Industry* (November): 16–19.

More questions about ISO 9000. 1993. *Continuous Improvement* (August): 2–4.

Paton, S. M. 1991. The Baldrige, the Deming, ISO 9000 and you. *Quality Digest* (August): 18–26.

Petrick, K. 1994. ISO 9000 and the environment—Competing interests. *European Report on Industry* (February): 21–23.

Rabbit, J. T., P. A. Bergh, and Y. Dror. 1993. Capture a quality image with ISO 9000. *INTECH Applying Technology* (April): 5–6.

Raymond, C. 1993. An afternoon with an admiral. *OEM Off-Highway* (November): 40–42.

Silver, C. H., Jr. 1993. Is your company being torn apart by teamwork? *OEM Off-Highway* (November): 16–20.

Skrabec, Q. R., Jr. 1994. Integrating quality control into your TQM process. *Quality Digest* (January): 66–70.

Smith, R. 1996. *The QS-9000 answer book*. Red Bluff, Calif.: Payton Press.

Stamatis, D. H. 1993a. FMEA fulfills prevention intent of ISO 9000. *Quality Systems Update* (September): 15–17.

———. 1993b. ISO implementation: A systematic approach. Paper presented at the 1st Annual International Conference on ISO 9000, 1–2 November, Lake Buena Vista, Florida.

———. 1995. Toward an automotive quality standard: Revisions of QS-9000 fall short of expectations. *Sensors: The Journal of Applied Sensing Technology* (November): 4–5.

———. 1995. QS-9000 revisions: Not far enough? *Quality Digest* (December): 6–8.

———. 1996. *Documenting and auditing for ISO 9000 and QS-9000*. Burr Ridge, Ill.: Irwin.

———. 1995. *ISO 9000 and implementing the basics to quality*. New York: Marcel Dekker.

———. 1996. QS-9000: A look at two clauses—4.1 and 4.2 *Quality Systems Update* (February): 9–20.

Stamatis, D. H., I. Epstein, and R. P. Cooney. 1993. Documenting personnel qualifications. *Quality Systems Update* (June): 21–23.

Stout, G. 1993. Quality practices in Europe. *Quality* (October): 6–7.

A strategy for standards and quality. 1992. *Quality at Work Newsletter* (November): 2–4.

Tartikoff, J. 1993. An environmental perspective on ISO 9000. Paper presented at the 1st Annual International Conference on ISO 9000, 1–2 November, Lake Buena Vista, Florida.

Teich, A. H. 1993. *Technology and the future.* New York: St. Martin's Press.

Tips on streamlining your ISO 9000 certification process. 1993. *Continuous Improvement* (December): 1–3.

Wolak, J. 1994. ISO 9000—A software market. *Quality* (March): 64.

Wayman, W. R. 1994. ISO 9001: A guide to effective design reviews. *Quality Digest* (January): 45–48.

Index